OUTRAGEOUS WOMEN OF ANCIENT TIMES

by Vicki León

John Wiley & Sons, Inc.

New York • Chichester • Weinheim • Brisbane • Singapore • Toronto

This text is printed on acid-free paper.

Copyright © 1998 by Vicki León
Illustrations copyright © 1998 by Lisa M. Brown
Maps copyright © 1998 by Jessica Wolk-Stanley
Designed by BTD/Robin Bentz and Ann Obringer
Published by John Wiley & Sons, Inc.

Poetry excerpts are reprinted by the kind permission of the following:

Sappho: from Fragment 105a, page 31, of *The Woman and the Lyre* by
Jane M. Snyder. Translation by Jane M. Snyder. Copyright © 1989 by the
Board of Trustees, Southern Illinois University.

Enheduana: from *The Exaltation of Inanna,* by William W. Hallo and
J.J.A. Van Dijk. Copyright © 1968 by Hallo and Van Dijk. Reprinted by
permission of Yale University Press.

LIBRARY OF CONGRESS CATALOGING-IN-PUBLICATION DATA
León, Vicki
      Outrageous women of ancient times / Vicki León.
        p. cm. -- (Outrageous women series)
      Summary: Recounts the stories of bold, notorious, or successful
women in such early cultures as ancient Greece, Mesopotamia, and
China.
   ISBN 0-471-17006-2 (pbk. : alk. paper)
    1. Women--History--Juvenile literature. 2. Civilization, Ancient-
-Juvenile literature. [1. Women--History. 2. Civilization,
ancient.] I. Title. II. Series
HQ1127.L43   1997
305.4'093--dc21   97-10836

Printed in the United States of America

10 9 8 7 6 5 4 3 2 1

TO VAL AND KEVIN

MY OWN WISE AND
SALTY HIPPARCHIA

AND HER RAGGED
PHILOSOPHER

C O N T E N T S

H ave you ever wondered what it would be like to go through life without a name of your own? Imagine being called "so-and-so's little girl" or "the blonde in the front row" your whole life. Your name gives you power and identity. It makes you an individual.

As a kid, I loved history, but teachers who rattled off history as a series of dates and wars left me cold. What I craved were flesh-and-blood people. Since half the kids in my class were girls, I expected that half the people we'd hear about would be female, too. Was I ever wrong! That early frustration, however, made me begin my own search. I set out to find the real women behind the statues of Greece and Egypt, the lives hidden behind all those endless dates and dull generalizations. I wanted to track down the women of long ago, to learn their stories. That's what I've done in this book.

As I dug deeper into early cultures, I found hundreds of bold women. Some were famous in their day for good deeds, some were notorious for bad ones. Others achieved something much better than fame: success in life, on their own terms.

My search wasn't easy. Even in our century, women often end up in the fine print or left out entirely. Nearly all the ancient writers were men, who liked to use stories about women as filler, before getting to "the good stuff" about wars and other men.

The stories I've unearthed about extraordinary women aren't always complete. Often we don't know the year they were born, or what they looked like. I've come to see that their lives resemble the Venus di Milo. This 2300-year-old work of art, the most famous statue in the world, is seen by millions of visitors to the Louvre in Paris each year. When visitors first look at the creamy, well-rounded body and face of Venus, the goddess of love, they're sometimes surprised to see that her right arm is broken off above the elbow and her left arm is missing entirely.

There are pieces missing from our women's lives. Sometimes the gaps are small. Other times, they're huge. But we can still enjoy and learn from what is left. After all, we don't put down the sublime art of the Venus di Milo because she is shy a few parts. Even when it's fragmentary, the real-life history of earlier women empowers us. It lets us know that we've had fearless foremothers for thousands of years, not just in our times.

Archaeology is one tool being used to fill the gaps about long-ago women of achievement. Some of the stories you'll read in this book have come from the spadework of archaeologists. Other female accomplishments, often thought legendary, have been proven by modern finds also. Researchers have learned to read the information hidden in coins, inscriptions on monuments or walls, artifacts of daily life, and more. Historians also study the inner workings of the culture in which a woman lived. I've drawn on all these things to tell the stories in this book.

Drawn from cultures as different as Vietnam and Rome, separated by thousands of years from us and from each other, what did these women share? Even as youngsters, they set out to do things, in societies (and often in families) that did not encourage independence. Their common bond is their daring—but each woman is as individual as a snowflake, as individual as her name. Together, they form a picture of our own selves as we might have lived, thousands of years ago.

THE DATING GAME IN DAYS OF OLD

People weren't always obsessed with time. Birthdays, for instance, meant little to ancient cultures. Folks kept track of time in a variety of ways. Years were named after a priestess's or an emperor's time in office, or for events like earthquakes or the Olympic Games. No one living long ago used "B.C." or "A.D." That system was invented by the Christian church, centuries after Christ. Wanting to set an official date for Easter, they worked backward to establish a firm date for the birth of Jesus. Anything before Christ's birth was called "B.C." Anything after was called "anno Domini" or "in the year of our Lord." (They were off by several years, as it turned out.) Jews, Moslems, Buddhists, and other cultures had their own dating systems as well. However, most books use the B.C./A.D. scheme, warts and all, to give a time reference that everyone is familiar with. Reluctantly, this book will do so also.

I

BRIGHT LIGHTS, BIG CITY

Rome

IF WE COMPARE *the spread of civilizations to plants, Rome resembled a strawberry. It began in what is now central Italy around 753 B.C. Its heart remained the city of Rome until the last gasp of its empire, around 476 A.D. As it grew from a tribe ruled by a king into a republic, Rome sent out its armies, like a strawberry plant sending out runners, to conquer other lands and run them as provinces. By the first century A.D., Rome and its tendrils, now an empire ruled by an emperor, circled the Mediterranean Sea. Rome stood for practical things: good roads, big buildings, law and order, and nice hot baths. The empire had a pretty relaxed attitude towards its millions of subjects. They could keep their own religions, language, and customs—as long as they paid taxes and never forgot who was boss.*

CHAPTER 1

Iaia of Cyzicus

(ACTIVE AROUND 90 B.C.)

She grew up in Cyzicus, a backwater town of Asia Minor (called Turkey today), more than a thousand miles from the artistic action, creative excitement, and prestige of Rome. Nevertheless, Iaia always knew she wanted to be an artist. Not just one of the *parietarii*—the anonymous artisans who worked on the backgrounds and details of murals and frescoes. No. She set out to be an *imaginarius*—a real painter, an artist recognized by name. The *imaginarii* had prestige. Besides doing paintings to hang on walls, they were paid to paint the walls themselves. Public places and rich peoples' homes glowed with their scenes, figures, and landscapes.

Few people got to be *imaginarii*. Fewer still had the talent so that their work got recognized by name. And no Roman woman had ever become a famous *imaginarius*. To become that one-in-a-million woman, Iaia realized that she would have to dedicate herself to her art. She took a vow never to marry. Iaia probably didn't have a mentor in her family, either—an artistic father or brother (or sister) to show her the ropes. But becoming an artist was worth any price. After studying her craft for years, the young painter finally felt ready to head for Rome.

Just getting safely to Rome must have been an adventure. Iaia left her pretty little hometown, perched on a peninsula that jutted into the Sea of Marmara, and traveled by land to Smyrna, the biggest port in Asia Minor. From there, she journeyed by sea to Ostia, Rome's port, a voyage of three weeks or so—if the winds were favorable.

Iaia quickly settled into big-city life. In addition to painting in oils, Iaia loved carving ivory. Using an engraving tool called the cestrum, she made tiny portraits in ivory that were very popular. Some of the portraits were for seal rings, a useful item nearly everyone wore or carried. Seal rings functioned as personal rubber stamps. People used their seals to "sign" documents. They pressed the

STATE OF THE ARTS

Rome in Iaia's day was wall-to-wall with creative people—most of them writers rather than painters, however. The most famous was Marcus Varro, a writer whose 490-book output made him the Stephen King of his day. Called "the best educated Roman," Varro ran the great public library and helped to create a favorable climate for all the arts. That helped people like Iaia and her two fiercest competitors, the painters Sopolis and Dionysius. Temples, galleries, and buildings around Italy were filled with the works of these artists. Iaia must have been the talk of the art world in Rome after she began to command higher prices than her male competitors!

rings into hot wax or soft clay; when the wax or clay dried, it left the unique design of the seal behind. Containers of precious goods, such as fine wines, also were sealed. If the seal was broken, it was a clue that someone had been sampling the contents!

Many rich Romans wore Iaia's work on their fingers. Sometimes her ivory miniatures were hung on a gold chain around the proud owner's neck. But Iaia's favorite medium remained painting. Starting with her native talent and adding a lot of hard work, Iaia gradually became well known. With fame came fancy prices; soon only the wealthiest could afford to hire her to paint their portraits. This couldn't have pleased the two leading artists of the day—both of them men. By 90 B.C. or so, eager art buyers were paying far more for Iaia's paintings than for pictures by her two male competitors. Not only did she get much higher prices for her work, but she wielded her brushes with an uncanny speed.

"Look at her hands!" people would marvel. "Such talent—and the swiftness of the god Mercury!"

Above all else, Iaia enjoyed painting women. One of her most talked-about pictures was a large panel painted on wood that she

~~~~~~

LOST IN THE TRANSLATION?

All through history, creative people like artists, actors, and writers have gone by "stage" or "pen" names. Iaia, for instance, was called Lala and Marcia by later historians. These other names may not have been Iaia's idea. Remember, this was before printing was invented. Scribes copied books by hand. Errors crept in, especially when one scribe couldn't read another's handwriting. At times, another word for "pen name" might be "mistake"!

~~~~~~

did of an old woman from Naples. Another huge success was her own self-portrait, done by using a mirror. (In Iaia's day, mirrors were small and made of polished metal; that made it more of a challenge to see yourself, much less paint your own picture.)

Sad to say, no examples of Iaia's work have yet been found. Our only description of her art comes from Pliny, a Roman author famous for his encyclopedia-like books. In our own century, however, an oil painting from the city of Herculaneum, buried by the volcanic eruption of Mt. Vesuvius in 79 A.D., was uncovered. Now hanging in the Naples Museum, this large oil depicts a female artist sitting at an easel, painting. Even if the subject is of another female artist, it gives us a clear picture of how Iaia, Rome's one-in-a-million *imaginarius*, might have looked as she worked.

TOOLS OF THE TRADE

Artists of ancient times usually painted on wood. Their biggest expense would have been paints. Some colors were rarer than others. Sky-blue came from a copper silicate in the Near East. Black came from wood or wine dregs, burned in an oven. The priciest color was a warm red, which people called "Pompeiian red" because it was often used on the frescoes in that Italian city. It came from a special kind of mercury ore, found in Spain and northern Asia Minor. Iaia and other painters had a way of making their colors more intense and glowing. They mixed each pigment with wax, then heated it before they painted with it—a technique called the encaustic method.

CHAPTER 2

Hortensia of Rome

(ACTIVE AROUND 42 B.C.)

Hortensia lived in a clean, warm, and well-fed world atop a high hill in Rome. Like other girls of the Roman aristocracy, Hortensia wore exquisite jewelry. Around her neck hung a heavy gold bulla, an amulet that showed her high social status. She had countless slaves and servants to dress her, fix her hair, go on errands, and give her massages. Her family had magnificent villas all over the place, including a seaside palace overlooking the Bay of Naples. There were parks surrounding the palace, with woods full of rare trees and exotic animals. And the grounds of Hortensia's seaside home held a series of ponds stocked with special fish for the table. The family wine cellar alone was bigger than many citizens' homes—it held over 10,000 casks of wine.

As was the custom for high-society girls, Hortensia studied at home with tutors—probably quite a few of them. She had a very bright and lively mind, and enjoyed her lessons in Latin and Greek literature, music, and history. She really took a shine to oratory—

what we'd call "public speaking" today. In addition to great orators from the past, like Demosthenes of Athens, she could study her own father's words. Over the years, Quintus Hortensius Hortalus had made many famous speeches at the Forum, the meeting place for political leaders, where he and another fast-talking orator named Cicero were big rivals.

When Hortensia turned thirteen or fourteen, she officially became an adult. In a traditional ceremony at the house, she took off her gold bulla necklace and carefully placed it on the lararium, the family altar to her ancestors. Not long afterwards, her father died. Still mourning her dad, she went on to marry a man named Sevilius Caepio, who also died a few years later, leaving Hortensia a widow.

Although Hortensia's personal environment was still the epitome of order and luxury, her homeland was being torn to bits by a series of civil wars. About 42 B.C., something major happened. At first it distracted Hortensia, now in her twenties, from her grief; later it pushed her into the limelight of history.

Her country was being run by three men: Octavian, Lepidus, and Marc Antony. These leaders, called triumvirs, had started yet another war against two of the assassins of Julius Caesar. War being a very expensive activity even back then, they needed more money. A new tax, perhaps. But what kind? And who would pay it? First they demanded money from certain very wealthy men. Then one of them had a bright idea: Let's tax 1,400 of the richest women in Rome!

In a flash, the triumvirs worked out their tax scheme. They would only go after the women whose annual income was over 100,000 denarii. The tax would be one year's income from each of them, plus a "loan" to the government of a percentage of their properties.

Romans hated taxes just as much as Americans do today, but they understood that in times of war or disaster, people had to chip in. Rich women had contributed generously many times already. In 390 B.C., the women of the city donated a thousand pounds of gold to get rid of the barbarians who had sacked Rome. Later, during the long and costly war the Romans had fought against Hannibal and the city of Carthage, women had made even greater sacrifices.

This time was different. It wasn't a war to defend their country. And the proposed taxes were going to be squeezed mostly from

A GIFT FOR GAB

Although very few women had professions in ancient Rome, the female way with words did offer an avenue for several besides Hortensia to become orators or lawyers. For instance, a woman named Gaia Afrania took the bold step of becoming her own attorney. She was married to a Roman senator and was a society woman. Nevertheless, her actions outraged the all-male crowd at the Roman Forum. They were still fuming over her, and writing nasty things about her, a whole century later!

the wealth of a few women. Every woman who fell in the 100,000-denarii bracket was in a rage. "We've got to fight this thing as a group," they said. Besides the power of numbers, they needed a spokeswoman to present their case. It was an easy choice. Hortesia, already well known as being "just like her dad" when it came to the law and public speaking, would be perfect. Hortensia for advocate! they cried.

Their first thought was to present their case to the female relatives of the triumvirs, and then to the rulers themselves. With Hortensia as their spokesperson, they approached the sister of one and the mother of another, who both agreed that the new tax was wrong. Then they went to see Fulvia, the second wife of Marc Antony. Her mind already made up, Fulvia wouldn't let the women in her door, and had them rudely pushed away by her guards.

Enough was enough. Now red-hot angry, Hortensia and the women she was speaking for marched noisily through the city, heading for the Roman Forum. Other Romans, upset at the sight of noblewomen being badly treated, followed them to the Forum, where a large crowd gathered. Women rarely entered the building where the political leaders met; when they did, it was by request. Hortensia, however, didn't stop. She pushed her way in, over the protests of the guards outside. With the other women at her heels, she calmly and clearly presented their case to Octavian, Antony, and Lepidus.

Although her exact words have not survived, we have a pretty close facsimile of her speech from a writer of the time. Among other things, Hortensia said, "Why should we pay taxes when we do not share in the honors, offices, military commands, or the government, for which you fight between yourselves with such harmful results? You say 'Because this is a time of war.' When have there *not* been wars? When have taxes ever been imposed on women, whom nature sets apart from men? Our mothers did make contributions when you were in danger of losing the whole empire and the city itself through the conflict with the Carthaginians. But they contributed voluntarily.

"Let war with the Gauls or the Parthians come, and we shall not be inferior to our mothers when it is a question of common safety. But as for civil wars—we will never contribute, and we will never help you fight each other!"

The triumvirs got worked up when they heard Hortensia. The nerve of these women and their demands! Hortensia had made

some good points; nevertheless, they ordered the guards to force the women from the room. When the crowd outside saw what was happening, they went wild. Hastily the triumvirs reversed themselves, saying that they would make a decision in twenty-four hours.

The next day, Hortensia and her colleagues got the word. Thanks to her spirited and sensible speech, the triumvirs had reduced the number of women to be taxed from 1400 to 400. But the most important point that Hortensia won was the issue of fairness. The tax was now going to fall on men and women alike. Hortensia may have been disappointed at part of the verdict, but it was a mighty victory all the same.

For years after that, everyone said admiringly, "The famous orator Hortensius lives again in the female line, and breathes in his daughter's words!" Today, the situation is reversed. No one remembers much about Hortensius—except as the father of Hortensia, the golden-tongued woman who won the most famous class-action case in Roman history.

CHAPTER 3

Locusta of Gaul

(ACTIVE 50 A.D.)

Female rags-to-riches stories and women who made it on street smarts have been around for ages. Locusta of Gaul, for instance, was a poor girl who made good. In her case, it might be more accurate to say Locusta was a poor girl who made good by making bad!

Her story began in first century A.D. Gaul, a part of the Roman Empire we'd call "France." Locusta could have been a war captive, and gotten to Rome that way. Then again, as a girl from the boondocks, she may have chosen to go to Italy to find a career.

Locusta had a background in herbal lore, and she turned that knowledge into gold. Did she open a health food store? Quite the opposite—she became a professional poisoner. At this time, Rome was filled with ambitious or greedy people who wanted to hurry along the deaths of their rich relatives or rivals—but wanted to make it look like natural causes.

Soon Locusta became the hit-woman of choice and had a long list of satisfied clients. She also had a long arrest record—one of the drawbacks of being a professional poisoner. However, since her customers tended to be bigwigs, Locusta neatly avoided the death penalty, and got out of jail quicker than you might expect.

Around 54 A.D., Locusta got a secret summons from the most important potential client she'd ever had. Delighted, Locusta hurried to meet with her. It was Empress Agrippina, the fourth wife of Emperor Claudius. Agrippina had big plans—she wanted to put Nero, her son by a prior marriage, on the emperor's throne of Rome. And she was tired of waiting for that old fuddy-duddy, the 64-year-old Claudius, to die. "I need your help, Locusta," she said.

A LONG PROUD LINE OF POISONERS

Locusta may have been the most notorious and professional poisoner Rome ever saw, but she was far from the only one. Four hundred years before her, Romans were glued to a sensational mass trial of twenty respectable married women—all accused of being poisoners. Their husbands and other relatives were dropping like flies, but the gruesome details of their deaths made it unlikely that it was an epidemic. The defendants said they'd been giving their loved ones a health tonic. When asked to prove it, all twenty drank down a sample of their brew in court—and died on the spot! The years 180 B.C. and 154 B.C also saw more female poisoners on trial. Two of them were found guilty. Because they were noblewomen, they got the "lightest" penalty: death by strangling!

The two women exchanged ideas. Naturally Emperor Claudius had food tasters, as did most emperors and their heirs in those touchy times. Locusta said she would prepare a new poison, wickedly strong but tasteless, and put it in a big batch of mushrooms. Then Agrippina would bring them to the emperor as a special treat. Claudius dearly loved mushrooms. Agrippina knew he wasn't terribly fond of her, but she didn't think he would refuse something from her own hand. To be on the safe side, she bribed Claudius' food taster to stay out of the way and then waited for the perfect moment.

MUSHROOMS, ANYONE?

One night when the emperor had no special company and his most protective, right-hand man was sick, the plan went forward. Quite tipsy with wine, the unsuspecting Claudius gobbled up the mushrooms. Locusta hadn't spared the toxic ingredients. Almost immediately, he started gasping for breath and lost his voice. Soon he doubled up with stomach cramps. He staggered from the table to his bed, Agrippina at his side, cooing with pretended concern.

In horrible pain, Claudius began to throw up, which gave his murderous wife some second thoughts. What if he got rid of the poison before it did its fatal work? She and Locusta had a backup plan, however. Agrippina (or possibly a doctor she'd bribed) gave Claudius another jolt of poison on a feather put down his throat. (Another version says she gave him a poison enema.) By the dawn of October 13, 54 A.D., Emperor Claudius was dead. By noon, the nearsighted 16-year-old Nero was proclaimed emperor.

Publicly, the new emperor called Agrippina "the best of mothers" and lavished her with honors. Locusta, however, became the official fall guy for Claudius' death. Charged with murder, she was tossed into prison and given a death sentence. Privately, Nero knew the part that Locusta had played in his becoming emperor. Months later, he quietly ordered her release. He had a new plan for her services.

Although he had anything-goes power over the Roman Empire, Nero still worried about a potential rival—Britannicus, Claudius' son from an earlier marriage. The boy was now fourteen. Jealous and fearful, Nero became convinced that Britannicus was after "his" throne. The boy needed to disappear. This time, however, it really had to look like a natural death.

Locusta knew, as Nero did, that Britannicus suffered from epilepsy and thought that his condition could be useful to the plan. Their scheme was to carry off the dirty deed in full view of everyone, at a family dinner. Nero, his mother, and his close relatives normally ate dinner reclining on couches, in the palace dining room. Each person, Britannicus included, had his own food taster.

That evening, the wine was brought in and poured into goblets. The boy's food taster tried the wine, then passed the goblet on to Britannicus. He took a sip, made a face, and handed it back. "It's too hot," he said. (Romans had an odd habit of diluting their wines with hot water.) The food taster then added some cold water into the wine—but he failed to taste the innocent-looking water, which contained Locusta's evil creation.

The instant Britannicus drank his cooled wine, his whole body went into sharp convulsions and he fell over backwards. He clutched his throat, not able to breathe or talk.

The children ran from the room; the grownups, shocked and afraid, looked at Nero. The emperor kept on eating, unperturbed. "Don't worry," he told the others. "Britannicus has the sacred disease—epilepsy. He'll soon come out of his fit and regain his sight and voice. Let's just enjoy the dinner—he'll be fine." He motioned for the servants to carry the boy from the room. After a brief pause, people began to eat and drink again, careful not to let their faces show any signs of terror, revulsion, or curiosity. Although she tried to keep her face calm, Nero's mom Agrippina was in agony. She knew exactly what had happened, even though she hadn't been consulted. Could she be next?

That same night, Britannicus died. A huge storm broke out; in spite of the weather, he was hastily buried in the pouring rain. Some people got a look at the boy, or said they did. They gossiped that his dead face, coated with chalk to hide the tell-tale blueish or reddish signs of poisoning, was washed clean by the rain, revealing the evidence of Locusta's and Nero's crime. No one was either brave or foolish enough to do anything about Britannicus, however.

After that, satisfied customer Nero began to make Locusta a wealthy woman. He gave her land, money, referrals, more assignments, and a full pardon for all poisonings (the ones she'd been caught at, anyway). Locusta soon did a rip-roaring business in poisonings for hire, and even started a school for would-be killers, where she taught the toxic arts.

There was one assignment Nero didn't give to Locusta, although maybe he should have. In 59 A.D., the emperor finally got up the nerve to assassinate his own mother, Agrippina. (Frankly, he was afraid that she would beat him to it someday.) Nero arranged for her to take a boat trip, and thoughtfully supplied the boat: a special model with a collapsible lead ceiling. This high-tech murder attempt failed. On his second try, he sent assassins with knives. They succeeded.

By now, however, everybody in the country knew what he had done. In its own way, the Roman Senate was as cowardly as Emperor Nero. They ignored his crime—and others that Nero committed—for nine years.

During this period, Locusta continued her own underworld business success. She even furnished Nero with a "secret agent" poison kit for himself, should he ever need it. And in 68 A.D., that day came. Given Nero's by-now rather long list of crimes, the members of the Roman Senate finally condemned him to death. Nero promptly ran away—but left Locusta's poison kit behind in the confusion. Just before he was caught, he used his dagger to kill himself, sighing, "What an artist dies in me!"

And what about Locusta? When a brand-new Roman emperor took the throne, she kept a very low profile. Later that year, however, this one-woman crime spree got asked out on a date she just couldn't wiggle out of—with the official state executioner.

II

SMALL TOWNS, BIG IDEAS

Greece and Turkey

BUOYANT, IMPULSIVE, AND *brilliant, the ancient culture of Greece resembled a dandelion in the way it spread. Until more modern times, "Greece" didn't really exist as a country. Rather, the Greeks formed themselves into small city-states called poleis. Each polis was a town or city that included the lands around it. The city-states fought nonstop; only the sacred truce for the Olympic Games every four years brought temporary peace.*

When a city-state like Athens or Corinth got too big, it sent its surplus people to found a new colony. These bits of Greekness scattered like dandelion fluff around the Mediterranean and Black Seas, forming city-states from North Africa to Asia Minor (now modern Turkey).

The rich coastlines and volcanic landscapes of Asia Minor, long a home to successive civilizations like the Hittites and the Persians, proved to be popular with Greek colonizers also. Glittering cities arose, prosperous and full of architectural wonders like the Temple of Diana at Ephesus.

Even after super-organizer Rome began to take over politically, things remained much the same throughout Greece and Asia Minor. People in the city-states still spoke Greek, enjoyed athletics, drank wine, and argued about politics, religion, and philosophy.

~~~~~~

CHAPTER 4

Sappho of Lesbos

(A C T I V E   6 0 0   B . C .)

S appho was a Lesbian. So were her mom, her dad, her three brothers, and even the wine served at her dinner table. How was that possible? Simple. Until the nineteenth century, "lesbian" just meant someone—or something—from Lesbos, a Greek island eight miles off the coast of Turkey.

Born somewhere between 640 and 600 B.C. to aristocratic parents, Sappho and her three brothers grew up in Eressos, a pocket-sized place that spilled down to the sea. It may have been tiny, but Eressos was one of the five ruling cities of Lesbos. Sappho's island offered a variety of landscapes where a dreamy young poet could lose herself. Well supplied with water, the island looked like a woman in a spring gown—greenly forested, polka-dotted with roses and violets and honey-lotus, the curves of its valleys and hills covered with apple trees, olive groves, and vineyards.

In this calm and beautiful setting, dark-haired Sappho ripened into a young woman who'd been singled out by the Muses,

~~~~~~

the nine goddesses of the arts. She loved to dance and sing. Soon she picked up and mastered the lyre (an early ancestor of the guitar) to accompany her clear, cool voice. She was small-boned, and her hands had a hard time playing the seven-stringed instrument. So Sappho invented a smaller lyre and then a special pick for it, called a plectrum.

Of all the things she loved to do, composing poetry was her passion. Poetry in Sappho's time was more like our music; it was almost always sung and accompanied by the lyre. That's why Sappho's verses are called "lyric poetry," and why the words to our modern songs are still called "lyrics." She wrote more than 500 poems for herself, for her friends, and for her students. Her words, as vivid as island sunsets, spoke of love and nature, ancient myths and family. For instance, here is part of a wedding song that Sappho wrote, describing the untouched quality of a new bride in a way that never would have occurred to most people:

Just like a sweet apple which ripens on the uppermost bough,
on the top of the topmost; but the apple-gatherers forgot it,
or rather, they didn't forget it, but they could not reach it.

With her burning talent, Sappho was a flame who drew other would-be poets like moths. Year after year, girls in their teens or even younger came from places hundreds of miles away, sometimes making a sea voyage, to study with her. The group they formed has no parallel with anything in our experience today. It was both innocent and sensual, an intimate circle of friends who exchanged ideas and emotions and loved one another dearly. It may be that Sappho and her friends were lesbian in the modern sense. It really doesn't matter. The love they felt for each other was genuine. The poetic fragments of Sappho, broken though they may be, are among the most treasured tokens we have from ancient times.

Some of Sappho's friends and pupils became famous poets in their own right. Damophila, whose home was on the Asia Minor mainland in distant Pamphilia, was one. Eventually she left Lesbos and established her own women's circle back home, composing love songs and hymns to the goddess Artemis in what came to be called "the Sapphic style."

THEIR CHURCH WAS THE GREAT OUTDOORS

Sappho also composed songs for choruses and pieces for religious festivals; she herself headed a cult of Aphrodite, the goddess of love. Such festivals were celebrated out of doors in Greece. In the spring, the unmarried girls would make pilgrimages to local shrines, singing and dancing in a leisurely procession, carrying flowers and other gifts for the god or goddess. Like the rest of Greece, Lesbos had shrines and temples everywhere. Some of the festivals were many miles from town, so Sappho and her friends might go there in horse-drawn chariots or carts decorated with flowers and pulled by oxen.

The image shows a sign reading "BUY 2 SAPPHO HEADS GET 1 FREE!!" and a banner reading "POETRY MONTH SPECIAL!"

TALL TALES OF THE RICH AND FAMOUS

Because she was an unforgettable figure, all kinds of gossip, legends, and tall tales attached themselves to Sappho, most after her death at about 550 B.C. One of the silliest came from Roman poet Ovid, who wrote a fictional poem about her over five centuries later. In it, an older Sappho fell in love with a gorgeous young man—and then in desperation killed herself by jumping off a cliff. The white cliffs where her leap supposedly took place are near the site of an old temple to Apollo, on the Greek island of Leukas. In Sappho's day, it was traditional for people to make a vow to the god Apollo. Then they took what was called "the holy leap." The high dive into deep water was not to commit suicide but to cleanse themselves of sin. Sappho's splash-down (if she made one at all) was a metaphorical leap to life.

Because Sappho's poetry is so centered around women, it's surprising to think of her with a husband. But she did have one: Cercolas, a wealthy man who hailed from the faraway Greek island of Andros. Her daughter Kleis, whom she described as "my heart's one pleasure," was the fruit of that marriage. Kleis was named after the poet's own mother. Sappho probably traveled with her husband on some of his business trips; it's known that she saw a great deal of Greece, meeting with other celebrated poets and impressing people great and humble.

One of the men she bowled over with her genius was Solon, a great lawmaker and leader of Athens and a poet of sorts himself. Once, at a dinner, Solon's nephew sang him one of Sappho's songs. Upon hearing it, Solon asked the boy to teach it to him immediately. When a dinner guest asked why, Solon said: "Once I learn it, I can die happy!"

Another of Sappho's fans was Plato the philosopher. Nearly two hundred years after her death, he wrote: "Some say there are nine Muses, but they're wrong. Look at Sappho of Lesbos; she makes ten."

Left a widow when she was barely in her forties, Sappho had other sad events in her life that became fuel for her poetry. She and her favorite brother quarreled bitterly and never made up. Her beloved island went through political turmoil, and Sappho had to leave her home and hide out in Italy for a time. (One poetry fragment of hers seems to criticize the political leadership of Lesbos, which may have led to her exile.)

In her lifetime, and for nearly a thousand years after, this nightingale of verse had a huge and devoted following around the Greek-speaking world. Her merchandising would have made

Michael Jordan jealous. Sculptors did a brisk business in "Sappho heads" and statues. Every educated person had books of her poems. Mytilene, the capital of Lesbos, used coins with Sappho's face on them for hundreds of years. There was even a mass market "Sappho the poet" likeness, which was painted on vases and walls and engraved onto gems.

Although as an artist she rated as highly as Homer and other famous male poets in ancient times, much of her poetry disappeared. Some of the loss may be due to a few Christian writers who were anxious to get rid of "pagan" influences like Sappho. Her poems, so direct and honest about love and passion, were looked on as bad examples. Even more of her output may have vanished during the later Dark Ages, when education took a nosedive and books were neglected.

As archaeologists know, however, stuff that has been thrown away often gets preserved by a quirk of fate. In the twentieth century, a couple of archaeologists named B.P. Grenfell and A.S. Hunt stumbled across some of the most complete versions of Sappho's poems yet found. These precious pieces of papyrus (an early form of paper) were buried, along with bits and pieces of other Greek books, in a thousand-year-old garbage dump in Egypt.

Hipparchia of Athens

(A C T I V E   3 3 0   B . C .)

Hipparchia and her husband, fellow philosopher Crates, lived on the streets of Athens around 330 B.C. You might call this couple the most famous homeless people in history. They survived on lentils cooked with herbs, barley bread, and water most of the time. They wore cloaks that also doubled as blankets to sleep on. And they raised two children in this lifestyle.

So how did a Greek girl from a well-to-do family in the northern provinces end up as a penniless philosopher on the busy streets of Athens?

Hipparchia's family had lots of money and connections in Maroneia, their hometown in the rainy green region of Thrace, hundreds of miles north of Athens. Kings stayed in Hipparchia's home; Philip of Macedon, the father of Alexander the Great, often lodged there while on war campaigns.

ATHENS, A PHILOSOPHER'S PARADISE

Many of the great schools of philosophy got their start in Athens. It had a lively intellectual climate. It had a great climate, period—which made it a wondrous walk-about town, the marble temples of its Acropolis shimmering like a spaceship above the city. In the fourth century B.C., Athens was home to the best art, the finest olive oil, the greatest chefs, the most argumentative lawyers, the liveliest culture, and the wisest philosophers. Among them were Socrates, Plato, Aristotle, and later, Epicurus. Hipparchia was not the only female philosopher. Dozens of women we know of, including Diotima, Themista, Aspasia, and Leontium, studied with the various schools of philosophy and became well known as teachers or writers.

Hipparchia and her brother Metrocles were very close. Avid readers, they adored philosophy. As kids, they spent time imitating the philosophers, asking questions of each other and arguing the pros and cons of the many different schools of belief.

Eventually, however, Metrocles went to the Academy in Athens to study philosophy seriously, at the university level. Hipparchia was happy for her brother, but she didn't see why she couldn't attend. After all, Greek women (a few, anyway) had studied for years at the Academy. A couple of them even became famous. Her parents pointed out that some of the female philosophy students had shady reputations. They were right. But Hipparchia made another point: it was the fact that women *did* things that shocked the Athenians and caused the scandalous talk. Respectable Athenian women were supposed to stay home, period. Athens might be full of wonderful philosophers, but people in that city had a thing or two to learn about the minds of women!

For several years, Hipparchia was stuck at home in Maroneia. Boys had started hanging around, attracted by her looks and her family background. The boys dropped hints about marriage. Her parents dropped hints about those who were good catches. She just wasn't interested.

Her days revolved around the letters she got from her brother. He'd started at the Academy, he wrote, then he'd switched to study at the Lyceum, the rival learning center started by Aristotle. As time wore on, his letters complained about the expense of being a student in Athens. Metrocles got a big allowance, but it wasn't enough. "Please send more money," he begged. "At the Lyceum, I have to buy fancy clothes, pay for my share of the wine and entertainment, and hire servants. Otherwise, I don't fit in."

Suddenly the letters from Metrocles stopped. Hipparchia and her parents were beginning to get seriously worried when a note arrived. In it, Metrocles said he'd now quit the Lyceum as well. He raved about his brand-new teacher—an extraordinary man named Crates. Relieved and curious, the family asked him to invite his teacher home on his next semester break.

When the two showed up, the parents did a double-take. Could this be the famous philosopher-teacher their son kept praising? They saw a hunchbacked, sunburnt fellow, an older man who wore a ragged and dirty cloak. Before long, though, Crates' kind ways and sense of humor made an impact. He had them in stitches

~~~~~~

OUTRAGEOUS AS A PHILOSOPHY: THE CYNICS

Cynic philosophers didn't wear the spotless white robes most sages wore. They didn't teach in a fine school or have paying pupils. The Greek word "cynic" (like our word "canine" from Latin) comes from the word for dog. Philosophers like Hipparchia "barked" about the hypocrisy and love of luxury in their world—and kept on "biting" their listeners with sharp words, sarcastic stories, and outrageous behavior. They believed that virtue was the main goal of life, but that very few people were virtuous. (Nowadays, we still call a person who believes that almost everyone is motivated by selfishness a "cynic.") Cynic philosophers used their shock tactics as a way to make people see, and think about, the invisible handcuffs that each society puts on its citizens.

~~~~~~

with his story about Metrocles, who'd adopted an all-bean diet to save money—only to have it backfire on him right in class! When Hipparchia's parents learned that Crates had gotten their son out of his deep depression over the incident, he really won them over.

Hipparchia didn't need winning over. She'd already embraced the Cynic philosophy of Crates, which she'd read about from her brother. The instant she saw Crates, she fell in love with the man himself. And she didn't try to hide it. "I want to marry him!" she said to her astonished folks. "And I swear, I'll kill myself if I don't get your consent!"

Even Crates tried to talk Hipparchia out of her passion. Although he felt the same way about her, he wasn't sure that this lovely girl from a privileged home could meet the challenges of his voluntarily poor, vagabond life.

"Look," he said. "I'll show you what you'll be getting if you marry me." With that, he took off his battered cloak, threw it on the floor, and stood nearly naked before her. "You're looking at the bridegroom and all his possessions," he said. "And unless you can share my style of life, it won't work between us."

Everyone in Athens gossiped about their partnership. Soon Hipparchia learned enough from her husband to take an equal role in their life's work: bringing advice, consolation, and help to people. With Crates, whose nickname was "Door Opener," she got a warm welcome at every home in the city. The young philosopher and her husband took a special interest in helping the working people and the poor, not merely the well-to-do.

She also met and studied with Diogenes, the crotchety old founder of Cynicism, who lived in a large clay jar (yes, a jar!) at the marketplace. He did comical things designed to make people

think. He was known to carry around a lighted lantern in the daytime. He would hold it up to people he met, saying he needed more light because he was "still looking for an honest man."

One of the most controversial things Hipparchia ever did was to go to dinner parties with her husband. (It was probably the only time she put on a nice gown or sandals from her old life.) These social events served as the most important nightlife in Athens, where witty conversation and clever remarks were as important as the drinks and dinner served. Athenian wives were left at home. Foreign women—that is, non-Athenian ones like Hipparchia—could attend, though few got invitations. Most often, the women asked to dinner parties were high-priced and well-educated courtesans or *heterae*. With her quick tongue and clever mind, Hipparchia more than held her own at these parties, loving the give-and-take of philosophical banter.

Athens bubbled with conflicting ideas about the nature of the universe, and Hipparchia learned from all of it. Besides raising a girl and a boy, teaching Cynic philosophy, and problem-solving for the people of Athens, she wrote various books and plays. So did her husband, Crates. Sadly, only a few bits remain—and they are his.

Hipparchia often heard Diogenes repeat a sentence that later became much quoted. "I'm a cosmopolitan," he said. "I am a citizen of the world." In her own way, she opened her horizons to become a global citizen. Although she had to oppose her parents and her society to do so, Hipparchia blazed a trail of female accomplishment through the toughest terrain of all—the usually for-men-only intellectual territory of classical Athens.

~~~~~~

DIFFERENT DRUMMER DIOGENES

Diogenes, the wise but cranky founder of Cynic philosophy, had a way of punching holes in meaningless grand gestures. For instance, once Alexander the Great made a quick stop to visit Diogenes. Standing in front of the humble clay jar where the old man sat sunning, the proud young man about to conquer the world asked, "Is there anything I can do for you? Anything at all? Just ask! I'll have it done."

"Yeah," said Diogenes. "Move out of my light."

Alexander laughed. Later, he often said, "If I could not be Alexander, I would want to be Diogenes."

By the way, Diogenes wasn't born poor. He chose poverty and his simple way of life, as did Hipparchia and Crates, who also came from monied families.

~~~~~~

CHAPTER 6

Hedea, Tryphosa, and Dionysia of Tralles

(ACTIVE 45 A.D.)

In the middle of the first century A.D., the Roman city of Tralles had three athletic superstars to brag about—all of them sisters. Hedea, Tryphosa, and Dionysia started out lucky. For one thing, their parents didn't leave them at the nearest temple after they were born. Unwanted girl babies were abandoned this way and left to die, or to be "adopted" as slaves. But our sisters were welcomed. Early in life, their father Hermesianax recognized their talents and made sure they got proper training.

Tryphosa, the oldest, and Dionysia, the baby, loved running more than anything. Both decided to work on the one-lap 200-meter footrace called the stade. They spent most of their time at the gymnasium, running on the soft dirt of the practice track. Since sandals were hard to run in, and gym shoes hadn't been invented yet, footracers always ran barefoot.

Hedea, the middle sister, could fly like the west wind on the track. She also had the best voice in the family, and could beat anyone at playing the lyre (an early relative of the guitar). But track and music events didn't seem like enough excitement for Hedea. She wanted to race war chariots, too.

Her father probably took some persuading. Horse racing was expensive and risky. Chariot racing was far riskier (that's why many owners "competed" by using hired charioteers). What Hedea wanted to do was the was riskiest of all. To compete in the war chariot event, you raced two (sometimes four) frisky horses around an oval track as fast as you could go—and you had to do this while standing in your chariot dressed in armor!

THE SPORTS-CRAZY TOWN OF TRALLES

Although the hometown of the girls sat far to the east of Rome in Asia Minor (we call that area Turkey today), Tralles had the feel of an important place. The buildings were handsome; the school of art and sculpture was famous. So were the local earthquakes, which flattened Tralles from time to time. When that happened, people just sighed and rebuilt bigger and better.

Like most other cities in the first century A.D., Tralles had its own gymnasium and public baths. These facilities were usually free. Everyone in town, not just the jocks, went there daily to work out, cleanse themselves, and catch up on the gossip.

Cities and towns like Tralles—Greek in language, thought, and culture—were dotted around the Mediterranean and Black Seas. The sisters spoke Greek and probably Latin, too—that was the "official" language of the Roman Empire, the political power in charge.

"Sure it's dangerous—but it's what I want to do, dad!" Hedea might have said. In any event, she stood her ground until he gave in. The girls trained hard. Besides exercise, their diet helped make them fit. Every day, they ate cheese, barley porridge, fruit, and the famous dried figs of Tralles. Back then, few people, athletes or not, ate meat every day.

These speedy siblings had a lot to get ready for. Competitive athletics was growing as fast as our computer industry is today. Six hundred years before the girls were born, there were only four Great Games, the most important being the Olympics. By Hedea's time, however, there were over 300 athletic meets each year, made possible in part by the peace the Romans had imposed on the Greeks and everyone else around the Mediterranean.

For nearly ten years, these young teens made a circuit of the most important games, traveling thousands of miles each year to compete at Delphi, Athens, Corinth, Argos, and other cities in Greece. (They may also have competed in Italy, Asia Minor, North Africa, and other sports-mad places where archaeologists have found evidence that women did indeed compete in athletics.)

By our trio's day, girls had begun to compete with boys some of the time. Here and there, athletic and musical contests were open to both, but we don't know whether the speedy sisters competed against girls or boys.

~~~~~~

GOING FOR THE GOLD—PAYDAY IN ANCIENT ATHLETICS

Hedea, Tryphosa, and Dionysia took part in two kinds of events: crown games and money games. Crown games, beginning with the Olympic Games in 776 B.C., were the oldest and most prestigious. Honors at the four major Crown games were mostly symbolic. The judges gave crowns of olive at the Olympics, wreaths of laurel at the Pythian, crowns of pine at the Isthmian, and wreaths of wild celery at the Nemean Games. At money games, winning athletes got cash and other gifts, paid for by the sponsoring city. The hometowns of the victors also showed their pride in many ways. Sometimes, officials would smash a huge hole in the defensive walls that circled their city. The returning athlete then rode through the hole in a chariot to lead a victory parade. "A city with a winner like this has no need of walls," the people said.

The sisters also had their own female role models for inspiration. The earliest footrace of all was not the Olympic Games, it was the Heraea, an ancient festival honoring the goddess Hera. The Heraean races were for young girls only. Every four years, barefoot teens dressed in short tunics competed at this sacred festival, run on the same site as the Olympic Games. First place winners got to put up their victory statues and inscriptions at Olympia, along with the Olympic winners.

~~~~~~

We do know that Tryphosa took laurel crowns at Delphi, at two Pythian Games in a row. She didn't rest on her laurels, either. (Even today, we use this 2,500-year-old expression.) Tryphosa followed her first victories with a celery crown at the next Nemean Games. She was the first girl to ever win those three golds. Dionysia, the youngest sister, grabbed the crown of pine at the Isthmian Games. Later, she won first prize at the Asclepeian Festival in Epidaurus.

Hedea triumphed at everything she tried. Competing at the Isthmian Games, she won the war chariot race. She also took two firsts for running at the Nemean and Sicyonian Games. On the music side, Hedea captured first prize in the girls' competition for lyre playing at the Sebasteia Festival in Athens.

Unlike our competitions today, the Greeks and Romans didn't believe in giving prizes for second and third place. Our trio no doubt took lots of seconds and thirds. Only their first place wins got recorded or rewarded, however.

Do we know what these early sports stars won besides symbolic crowns of laurel, pine, and wild celery? Cash prizes for certain: that's what would have been handed out at the Sicyonian, Asclepeian, and Sebasteian Festivals. The money was accompanied with gift mementos like silver cups, leather jackets, and beautiful vases filled with oil. Hedea, Tryphosa, and Dionysia were also made honorary citizens of other cities, such as Corinth, Delphi, and Athens. Honorary citizenship gave more perks, from tax-free pensions to free meals for life. Last but certainly not least, the sisters got to place statues of themselves at the shrine of the god Apollo at Delphi, the most sacred place on Greek soil. Besides its religious importance, Delphi was the International

Hall of Fame for great athletes, musicians, intellectuals, and other famous people.

The victory statues of the girls have vanished. However, the dedication made by their proud dad, with their career highlights written on it, still exists as proof of their astonishing deeds.

We don't know what happened to the three sisters after they retired from competition. They probably got married and had kids, as most people did. But their achievements, their flying feet, their chariot daring, and their musical talents remained an inspiration to other girls for centuries.

TROPHIES, TRIBUTE (BUT NO ENDORSEMENTS) FOR THE TRACK TRIO FROM TRALLES.

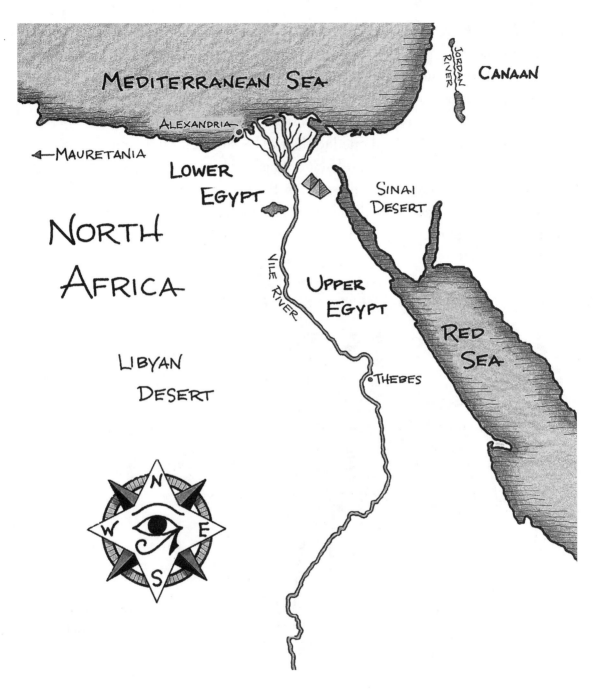

III

PYRAMIDS ARE FOREVER

Egypt and Northern Africa

AN EXCELLENT SYMBOL FOR *ancient Egypt would be a palm tree: tall and slender, with its roots in Africa and its leafy fronds branching into the Nile River delta, toward the Great Green. (Great Green was the name that the ancient Egyptians gave to the Mediterranean and the Red Seas.) Palm trees have a long life and look much the same from season to season. So, too, was ancient Egypt. Its people, civilized and organized for over 3,000 years, didn't like surprises. They worshiped order and tradition. They loved the predictable ebb and flow of the Nile that watered crops and fed people; the great pyramids, where pharaohs and queens slept for eternity; the glittering desert whose burning sands kept most invaders out of their lands. All these things gave comfort and meaning to the Egyptians of long ago.*

CHAPTER 7

Hatshepsut of Thebes

(ACTIVE AROUND 1500 B.C.)

A s a child, Hatshepsut sat on her father the pharaoh's lap, watching the Nile River as it moved past the windows of their simple mud palace at Thebes. After farmers harvested the crops, the waters would begin to rise, cool and green at first, later turning red and muddy as the sun grew hotter and the days got longer. At flood time, she and her brothers often went picnicking and sailing on the river. But the water Hatshepsut most longed to see and explore was the Great Green—the name the Egyptians gave to the sea. They believed that the Great Green circled Egypt like a huge watery serpent.

Water played a big part in Hatshepsut's life. When she was a young teen, her brother Wadjmose got caught in the rushes of the Nile while swimming, and he drowned. Before the seventy days of Wadjmose's embalming were up, Hatshepsut's only other brother died of fever. Her anguished father, Pharaoh Tutmose the First, ran to name her half-brother as the next pharaoh. Then he insisted that Hatshepsut marry her half-brother Tutmose Two, even though he was merely the son of a harem woman. In order for Tutmose to be accepted as pharaoh, he needed to marry the oldest daughter of a reigning king. The royal blood, as everyone knew, ran through the women. Unhappily Hatshepsut obeyed her dad's order.

Two days after her marriage, her father the god-king of Egypt fell dead. Hatshepsut became Great Queen at the age of thirteen, and wife to a sickly eight-year-old boy she couldn't stand.

For a time, however, being married didn't change things very much. She and Tutmose co-ruled with the help of the royal council. Hatshepsut kept on with her lessons in reading, writing, math, and history. She especially loved history, and avidly read the stories

MIRROR, MIRROR

Hatshepsut was slender and tiny—about five feet tall. When she looked at herself in the polished metal plate the Eygptians called a "see-face," she saw a high forehead, a small pointed chin and almond eyes of brown. She had the Tutmose family nose. She cared about her looks; like other women, she wore malachite green eyeliner and kohl around her lashes. As an adult, Hatshepsut may have been bald. Men and women, especially the higher classes, often shaved their heads and wore elaborate wigs instead. Hatshepsut may have been proudest of her skin; her smooth golden body got daily massages with scented oils. Her special favorite was called oil of ani. It must have smelled good; an inscription on one of her monuments says: "her fragrance was like a divine breath, her scent reached as far as the land of Punt."

of Egypt's past pharaohs. In the 1,400-year line of her country's rulers, only two or three women had ruled the country on their own. Hatshepsut thought that was very unfair. She had dreams, but she kept them to herself.

When Tutmose grew into a teen, he and Hat had two daughters. Other than that, Tutmose kept out of his wife's way for fourteen years. Although never very healthy, he went on long military campaigns to Nubia in the south, and Syria to the northeast. Around the palace, everyone knew their "co-rule" was on paper only; Hat made most of the decisions.

Tutmose lived barely into his thirties. Before his death around 1504 B.C., he openly showed his dislike of his wife's energy and ambition. To put the brakes on her, he named his only son Tutmose Three (a baby whose mother was from the harem, as his had been) as the next pharaoh.

Hatshepsut was angry. She knew that she had the brains, the blood, and the background to rule on her own. Still, it felt wonderful not having a husband to answer to. Quickly she jumped into the work of being queen and regent for baby Tutmose Three. She had several reliable officials to help. Ineni, who'd been palace chief in her father's time, was a rock. Soon she'd won over the powerful members of the royal council. Within several years of becoming queen, focusing her brains, persuasive powers, and ambition like a laser, Hatshepsut became what no other woman had ever become: the god-king of Egypt, a female pharaoh.

It happened gently, this revolutionary event in a land that didn't like change. Hatshepsut had planned her strategy for a long time. By blood, she had more claim to the pharaohship than anyone, male or female. But to win full acceptance among the priesthood, the nobles, and the people of Egypt, she needed powerful symbols to confirm her.

With the help of her architect and advisor Senenmut, a humbly born newcomer as ambitious as she was, she began work on a marvelous temple. Egypt already had lots of temples.

"This one's different," Hat said. "It's a garden for the god Amun. He was my father, you know." (Pharaohs often claimed kinship with the gods—it made them more divine.) The three terraces of Hat's new temple, glowing white against the coral-colored cliffs at Deir el-Bahari, made it one-of-a-kind in Egypt. On its walls, the female pharaoh directed Senenmut to carve pictures of herself as a child, being crowned as king of Egypt. In the pictures, she

HAT'S NEW TEMPLE TO HER "FATHER," THE GOD AMUN.

The Metropolitan Museum of Art, photograph by Egyptian Expedition.

The Metropolitan Museum of Art, Rogers Fund and Edward S. Harkness Gift, 1929. (29.3.2)

showed her mother being visited by the god Amun, and herself being chosen by the god to be king.

Hatshepsut knew the power of other symbols, too. She took to using the five potent titles carried by every pharaoh. Three of hers were: "King of Upper and Lower Egypt;" "Truth is the soul of Re;" and "She who embraces Amun, the foremost of women." She also wore the power clothes of a pharaoh. She dressed in a kilt, put on a male headdress, and even hung the fake "beard of wisdom" from her chin, as every pharaoh did. Then she paid artists and sculptors to make huge numbers of statues and murals of herself as pharaoh, and put them on display throughout Egypt. Soon people accepted her as a female king—although they still stumbled over exactly what to call her male majesty.

Although very happy with her success, Hatshepsut decided to do one more thing to convince her people that she was meant to lead. In Egypt and elsewhere in the ancient world, people consulted higher powers about important events in their lives. To get in touch with the gods, kings and commoners alike used oracles. Hat decided to consult the boat-oracle of the god Amun, her "father."

That year, at the Festival of the Western Valley, everyone gathered as usual along the banks of the Nile to watch the god's image get ferried across the river on a beautifully decorated barge. When the boat carrying the Amun figure was removed from the water, thirty-two priests

HAT'S MEN CARRY SPICE TREES, BABOONS, AND OTHER PRECIOUS CARGO FROM THE LAND OF PUNT UP THE GANGPLANK.

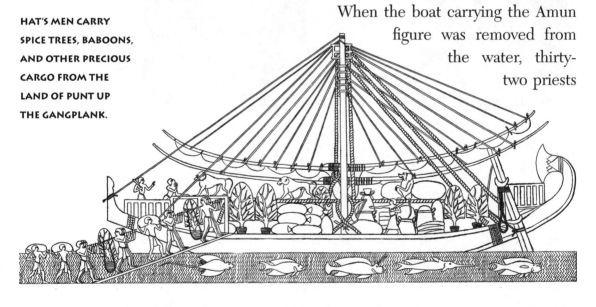

lifted it onto their shoulders. As the procession passed the female pharaoh on its way to the temple, the image of Amun nodded mysteriously toward Hatshepsut, indicating that it was the god's will that she should rule. Spectators went wild. Quickly, word of the miraculous event passed along the route of the oracle. (It's possible that the oracle nodded on its own. However, since the image was carried by priests who worked for Hatshepsut, there may not have been anything too mysterious about the god's favorable vote!)

Her reign legitimized, Hatshepsut turned eagerly to the projects she wanted to carry out. She organized a huge exploration and trade expedition to rediscover the land of Punt, a legendary place down the east side of Africa. No one from Egypt had been there for many generations. The ancient canal dug by earlier pharaohs from the delta region to the Red Sea had filled up. Hat, still itching with curiosity about the salty waters of the Great Green, sent a fleet of ships to Punt. Within a year, the voyagers returned in tri-

A WOMAN, A PLAN, A CANAL

Long before Hatshepsut's reign in the fifteenth century B.C., one of her pharaoh ancestors had carved a canal nearly 100 miles long, from the Nile River to the Red Sea. Over the centuries, it had silted up and become useless. When Hatshepsut came along, she looked into this dimly remembered feat, and said, "We need direct ship access to the sea. Let's make the canal open to the Great Green once again." And it was done. Many centuries later, Roman Emperor Nero tried to imitate Hatshepsut's feat. He failed. Finally, in 1869, a new canal called the Suez was dug by French engineers and called "a marvel of the nineteenth century."

umph, loaded with animal skins, rare woods, ivory, and spices like myrrh, which the Egyptians used by the ton as fragrant offerings in their temples. More than once, the female pharaoh must have wished that she could go on those daring expeditions. But she had to be content with tales and drawings of the Great Green, and of Punt's exotic lands, filled with frankincense trees and governed by a short, eccentric queen named Ety.

Hat sent out more trade expeditions to Africa and Palestine, which brought back turquoise for jewelry, wild beasts for the zoo she was setting up at her "Garden of Amun" temple, and other treasures. All these things and more were needed for her building program, carried out by the faithful Senenmut. Besides his architectural and managerial skills, he was Hatshepsut's lifelong confidant and tutor to her older daughter, Nefrure. It's often been speculated that Senenmut was Hat's lover. It's true that neither of them married; it's also true that she showed affection for him. But Hatshepsut was too shrewd a ruler to jeopardize her somewhat shaky standing as a divine female pharaoh by forming a permanent alliance with a commoner, no matter how uncommon he was.

Hatshepsut may have hoped to see her daughter on the throne after her. In the meantime, she gave Nefrure responsibilities—not all of them pleasant. She made her daughter a special priestess called the Divine Wife of Amun. Hat also forced her to marry Tutmose Three, the boy who'd been named the heir years ago. Now a teen, he was getting impatient for some real work. Like his father before him, Tutmose spent much time with the army as he got older, trying to capture foreign territories for Egypt.

As the years rolled by, and the Nile flooded and receded, Hatshepsut put her own stamp upon the land. She encouraged gold mining in the south of Egypt and the development of new ideas in sculpture. In her day, papyrus came into common use for texts like *The Book of the Dead*. She was especially proud of the obelisks (tall, narrow shafts of stone) she erected. (At the temple of Karnak near modern-day Luxor, one of them still points to the heavens: a spire of deep-red granite, at nearly 97 feet the tallest standing obelisk in Egypt.)

Even among the stability-loving Egyptians, all things must come to an end. In Hat's case, it was her pharaohship. Solo rule was so cool, she'd left Tutmose Three on hold for over twenty years. Patient at first, gradually Tutmose began to lobby for the top job; and at some point his wife Nefrure, who may have been a calming influence, died.

Hat might have stepped down gracefully; given her personality, it doesn't seem likely. One of the first things Tutmose did when he became pharaoh around 1483 B.C. was to scrub Egypt clean of Hatshepsut's name. Or try, anyway. Some of her statues he threw into a quarry. On other monuments and inscriptions, he (or his successors) had her name hacked out.

But the memory of Hatshepsut and her deeds as Egypt's female pharaoh refused to disappear. Now, after centuries of neglect, archaeologists and historians have renewed interest in her life; their work has brought more evidence of Hat's legacy to light. Thirty-five centuries after her death, admiration for this energetic leader now gleams like the gold that once covered her dazzling obelisks.

~~~~~~

Cleopatra Seven of Egypt and Cleopatra Selene of Mauretania

(ACTIVE 69 B.C. - 10 A.D.)

Cleopatra! The one ancient name that everyone knows. People usually think of her as a gorgeous Egyptian queen who used sex appeal to get her way. Cleo had many secrets to her success, but cover-girl beauty wasn't one of them. By the time she reached thirty, she even had a goiter under her chin. It's true that she wore fabulous pearls, had an actress's sense of timing, and used perfume as a secret weapon. Her allure, however, didn't depend on any of these things.

The first surprise about the Cleopatra we think we know is that she wasn't the first—or even the last—royal Cleo. She was number seven. For 250 years, her ancestors (Cleos one through six plus several without numbers) had been clever, often ambitious women. But Number Seven had these qualities and much more. Called Netjeret-merites, or "Goddess, Beloved of Her Father" by her Egyptian subjects, and Queen Cleopatra the Seventh by everyone else, she and her young brother took the throne as co-rulers

~~~~~~

after her alcoholic father died. It was 51 B.C., the year she turned seventeen.

A ruler whose blue blood was Macedonian Greek rather than ancient Egyptian, Cleo came from a long line called the Ptolemaic dynasty. She really knew how to communicate, and understood the power of relating to a person in his or her own tongue. An admiring writer of long ago said about her, "It was a pleasure merely to hear the sound of her voice, with which, like an instrument of many strings, she could pass from one language to another." Thanks to her quick mind and linguistic gifts, she used her melodious voice to talk to Romans, Greeks, Jews, Arabs, Persians, Ethiopians, and Egyptians in their own languages. In fact, Cleopatra was the first ruler in 475 years who bothered to learn the local dialect.

Young as she was, Cleo was a power player. In her career, she didn't shrink from eliminating her rivals—including her sister and her younger brothers, Ptolemys 13 and 14. And she was a cool-headed gambler with a global outlook. Through her personal relationships, first with Roman leader Julius Caesar, and later with Marc Antony, she had an Internet-sized goal. She wanted to link

CLEOMANIA

"Cleopatra" began as a personal name, but it became a dynastic (or generic) name for queens. That's why so many Macedonian Greek royal women carried it. The very first royal Cleopatra was nicknamed "the Syrian" for the real estate she brought to her marriage with Ptolemy Five. It's her name that is on the famous Rosetta Stone, the bilingual key that unlocked the secrets of the Egyptian hieroglyphics. Cleos two and three were mother and daughter queens of Egypt. Between them, they married three more of the line of ruling Ptolemy men and gave birth to additional baby pharaohs, each fatter than the one before. Other royal Cleos weren't as ambitious or as lucky. And a few royal Cleopatras even ended up being murdered by other Cleos in the family!

It's easy to see why Cleopatra the Seventh wanted a connection to Rome; that's where the power was. But why were Julius Caesar and other Romans so interested in Egypt? Bread and circuses. Egypt provided nearly all the wheat for Rome's daily bread, given out free to a huge number of people. To be popular, leaders also put on free "circuses" as well. The circus covered a variety of events, most of them sickeningly violent, such as gladiator fights and contests between wild beasts and condemned men. Besides being Rome's breadbasket, Egypt supplied wild beasts for the Roman circuses and even sand to cover the floor of the circus arenas. (The word "arena" means sand in Latin.)

the countries around the Mediterranean into a new world order, so that there would be a political partnership of East and West instead of an empire dominated by Rome. Since she was a Greek by blood and culture, and the ruler of Egypt too, Cleopatra planned to represent the Greek and Eastern partners in this "dream team" alliance.

Part of Cleopatra's appeal was her changeable nature. She could be serious and smart—or a wild and crazy party animal. She loved to read. And she could read people as well as books. That was how she won the loyalty of two very different Roman leaders. Her ability to become the woman for any occasion was not play-acting, however. Cleopatra had many facets to her personality; bold but not impulsive, quick-witted, full of energy and life, she also let her sincere feelings of love show.

When Julius Caesar, a smooth and experienced man in his fifties, came to Egypt looking for money and political support, 21-year-old Cleopatra quickly got his attention. She had herself concealed in a carpet, carried into his room, and rolled out at his feet. Julius was won over in a flash. Not only did he back her to rule Egypt instead of her brother, he fell for Cleopatra in a big way. Soon they were living together in the palace at Alexandria and she had a baby on the way. To make her child's parentage clear to everyone, Cleo called her son Ptolemy 15 Caesar. Everybody else nicknamed him Caesarion or "little Caesar."

In 45 B.C., big Caesar took Cleopatra and Caesarion to Rome, even though he had a wife there. He built a new temple to

Venus and presented Cleopatra as a goddess to the people. Her golden statue adorned the temple; coins soon appeared, showing Cleopatra as the goddess Isis-Venus. Julius intended to marry the Queen of Egypt. Together, they planned to rule the lands around the Mediterranean, and to make their young son leader some day.

Their grand plans came to a bloody end, though. Most locals didn't like the influence that the glamorous foreigner had on their leader. Alarmed Romans also saw Caesar as a power-grabbing dictator who had ended what was left of the Roman republic—and so a group of conspirators assassinated him.

Grabbing her son, Cleo quickly ran from Rome to Egypt. For three years she kept a low profile and studied the changing political scene. In 42 B.C., three Roman leaders divided the empire into segments. A likeable general named Marc Antony got control of the eastern lands.

Cleopatra wondered whether she could work with Marc Antony to pursue her dream of an East-West alliance. Marc made the first move. He asked Cleo to meet with him. As a fan and follower of Julius Caesar, he wanted to know which side she'd supported after Caesar's death. He also saw that Cleo's son with Caesar could be an important contender for leadership someday.

When the two met to negotiate, Marc caught her scent before he saw her. Cleopatra arrived in her floating palace, a perfumed barge with purple sails whose walls and floors were covered with roses. Her hands gave off the scent of kyphi, a rare mix of violets and other flower essences. Her feet were anointed with egyptium, an almond oil lotion with ingredients that included cinnamon and orange blossoms. Marc must have become intoxicated even before she served the wine!

Right away, however, Cleopatra saw that Marc wasn't like Julius. He wasn't bowled over by the sex kitten approach. He preferred to kid around, drink hard, and play practical jokes, like his soldiers. She immediately joined in the fun and behaved like one of the guys. Before long, their feelings turned deeper. First lovers, they eventually married, but their Egyptian wedding was never official in Roman eyes. In fact, Marc Antony had several Roman wives, and was technically a bigamist most of his life! In 40 B.C., he and Cleopatra had twins, a girl and a boy. Four years later, they had another son, whom they called Ptolemy Philadelphus.

Except for periods when Marc was absent, their family life was close-knit. Cleo and Marc took the kids along wherever they traveled, along with a whole entourage of servants, friends, celebrities, and groupies. They had homes in Egypt, Asia Minor (now called Turkey), and on the Greek island of Samos. Cleo was a loving mom; only the finest teachers were good enough for her kids. Between 36 B.C. and 31 B.C., the family shared many happy times.

In 31 B.C., Cleopatra and Marc's struggle with Rome came to a head. War could not be avoided. After Cleopatra contributed 200 ships and much money, she and Marc squared off with Octavian, their Roman rival, in a huge sea battle. In spite of their efforts, they lost. Things went downhill from there, and soon Octavian's armies were at the city gates of Alexandria. Cleopatra barricaded herself inside her treasurehouse, which was also her mausoleum. After receiving a garbled and untrue report that his love had committed suicide, a heartbroken Marc Antony plunged a sword into his body. Cleopatra's slaves managed to bring him to her place of refuge, where he died in her arms.

Cleopatra tried to negotiate with Octavian, the new leader of the Roman Empire. He didn't go for it; he had big plans to march her through the streets of Rome in his victory parade. She might have been grieving for Marc, but Cleopatra still had her wits about her. She and her servants obtained a couple of asps, sacred and deadly snakes, as a way to commit suicide. When Octavian's men broke into her quarters, they found Cleopatra dead, lying in state, dressed in her jeweled and perfumed best. Her female servants lay dying at her feet. Octavian was furious. Nevertheless, her daring global gamble fascinated him, as it still fascinates us.

With the deaths of Cleopatra Seven and Marc Antony, the independence of Egypt also vanished. The Romans took it over as a province.

But another Cleopatra survived. Remember the twins? They were named Cleopatra Selene (after Selene, the Greek moon goddess) and Alexander Helios (after the sun god). As a small girl, Cleo Selene sat on a golden throne, and was given vast lands in North Africa and the island of Cyprus.

After her mother and father died, Cleo Selene, her twin Alex, and their younger brother Ptolemy Philadelphus were brought to Rome. She and her brothers had to walk as golden prisoners in the victory parade of emperor Octavian. In spite of that humiliation, Cleo Selene and her brothers found themselves in a warm new home. Their adoptive mother? None other than good-natured Octavia, one of the widows of Marc Antony!

When Cleo Selene turned sixteen or so, she married Juba, who'd just been made the new king of Mauretania, a huge land in Northern Africa. He also had been taken to Rome as a youngster and educated there. The two were extremely well-suited. Studious

Cleo Selene loved books and languages. So did Juba. He became an author who wrote books on the geography of Africa and the nearby islands.

Together, Cleo Selene and Juba ruled Mauretania. Their kingdom began with the Canary Islands in the Atlantic Ocean, and ran east, clear across the countries we call Morocco, Algeria, and part of Libya. Cleo Selene still ruled the lands given her when her mother was alive; they continued to be called hers.

At their fine palace in their capital city of Caesarea, Queen Cleo collected Greek art and supported Greek cultural projects. She also loved children and had two boys of her own. Unlike her famous mother, Cleo Selene didn't care about uniting the world, or even ruling more than a corner of it. She and Juba enjoyed a long and peaceful reign. And when she died, the Cleopatra name and bloodline ended. Ended, yes, but didn't vanish. Even today, the very name "Cleopatra" is an icon, a legend, and the stirring symbol of a strong woman.

CHAPTER 9

Mary Prophetissa of Alexandria

(A C T I V E   I N   T H E   F I R S T   C E N T U R Y   A . D .)

Prophetissa" probably wasn't Mary's real last name. "Mary" may not have been her first name, either. When she began her career as an alchemist in the ancient city of Alexandria, Egypt, she used more aliases than a bank-robber in the Wild West! Besides "Prophetissa" or "Prophetissima," (which means best of prophets) she sometimes went by "Mary of Cleofa" or "Maria the Jewess." At other times, she was referred to as "Marie of Alexandria" and even "Miriam, sister of Moses." Although she might have used magic formulas in her work, Mary was no underworld figure. So why did she have so many nicknames?

Using different names, even adopting the name of a holy person from the past, was part of the mystery and magic of alchemy, the early ancestor of modern chemistry. In Mary's case, she probably was a mix of the ethnic groups—Jews, Greeks, Romans, Persians—that made the neighborhoods of Alexandria so interesting.

Her appearance is as much a mystery to us as her highly secretive occupation. It's a good guess, though, that Mary had dark hair, olive skin, and long-lashed brown eyes, made more brilliant with a bit of kohl eyeliner—just like so many of the women pictured in Egyptian funeral portraits at that time. Like them, she may have worn fine linen garments trimmed with borders of saffron or crimson, and earrings that twinkled with gems or pearls. In Mary's case, however, such finery would have only been for special occasions.

Most of the time, Mary spent her days cooped up in a dark, hot, smelly laboratory. Although she would have argued otherwise, she really was on a wild goose chase: to find the Philosopher's Stone, a substance that would turn lead and other metals into gold. Her competition with the countless other alchemists in Alexandria and around the ancient world was deadly serious, because the stakes were so very high. That's why Mary and her colleagues used different names, disguised their findings in symbolic language, and tried to keep their work a secret.

Although she (and everyone else) failed to find the Stone, Mary became a gem of an inventor. Working in her lab, she dreamed up the double boiler as a source of gentle, even heat for her experiments. Later, that double boiler made generations of cooks and pudding lovers happy. In fact, for nineteen centuries, her contribution has been called a "Mary's bath" by cooks in Italy, France, Spain, and other European countries.

ALCHEMY, THE MISSION IMPOSSIBLE OF ANCIENT TIMES

In the first century A.D., people had many different theories about how the natural world worked and what it was made of. Alchemists like Mary thought that each tiny piece of matter had a spark of the divine in it, called "pneuma" or "breath." The quest of the alchemist was a cross between a spiritual search for a holy grail and a scavenger hunt. Everybody's goal was to locate a primal substance called the Philosopher's Stone, which, people believed, could turn lead and other metals into gold.

One experiment led to another. While investigating the way in which poisonous substances interact with metals, Mary came up with another device. She called it a *kerotakis*; it had a shape like a lemonade jug. Inside its cylinder, she hoped, vapors from mercury, arsenic, and other substances would combine with metals. After the first try, she carefully opened the container. The vapors had definitely combined with the metal! Instead of gold, however, Mary saw that her device had caused lead and copper to combine in a new way. That combination, called an alloy, proved to be highly useful to science. Her alloy is still referred to as "Mary's Black."

Perhaps the most unexpected and valuable invention Mary made was something she called the *tribikos*. This three-part contraption, made of copper tubing, ceramic pottery, and metal, was the first true still. When heated, vapors from plant material and water would condense on the inside of the still, then trickle down and collect in a bottle. Using Mary's still, later experimenters had

ALEXANDRIA, THE INVENTOR-FRIENDLY CITY

Alexandria was a great place for inventors, scientific explorers, and alchemists. The steam engine, the piston, the water organ, and the syringe were all invented here. The city had a huge research university and library called the Museum. It also had a long tradition of craftsmanship. Working for the pharaohs and later rulers, local craftspeople made metalworking, ceramics, glass-blowing, and jewelry making into fine arts. Over the centuries, artisans developed many special tools and techniques—which alchemists like Mary borrowed for their own mystical quest.

a device to distill alcohol and essential oils. Her invention became the key to making liquors, perfumes, and many other substances.

Even though her inventions weren't exactly what Mary set out to do, she came to realize their value. At a certain point, probably late in her life, this ingenious female alchemist wrote a book, perhaps several books, about her experiments and discoveries. Her book, called *The Dialogue of María and Aros on the Magistery of Hermes*, was studied for centuries by medieval writers and alchemists, especially among the Islamic Arabs. Fragments of other books, such as *Maria Practica* and *The Gold-Making of Cleopatra*, preserve bits and pieces of Mary's work to the present day, including a drawing of her famous still.

Like alchemy itself, a tangy and unpredictable blend of magic, religion, philosophy, and science, Mary and her alchemist rivals provided the necessary ingredients for the first true chemistry labs of ancient times. Their work seldom led to gold or riches. Instead, it led to places and purposes far more exciting and worthwhile.

IV

SPIRITUAL
CRADLE

The Middle East

JEWS BORN IN THE *modern state of Israel are called sabras, meaning cactus. Like the plant, they're prickly and tough on the outside, soft on the inside. The cactus makes a good symbol for the people of the Middle East, which includes Israel and Syria. Although holy to Moslems and Christians as well as Jews, the area has seen little peace in its 3,000-year history. Nevertheless, like the sturdy cactus, people of this region have endured.*

To the east of Israel and Syria lies the region of Mesopotamia, the original Garden of Eden. More like a willow tree than a cactus, for five thousand years the region of Mesopotamia has yielded to one culture, then another. The hard-working Sumerians settled in first. Fond of barley beer and building stepped pyramids called ziggurats, the Sumerians built handsome city-states like Kish, Ur, and Mari. Eventually their culture gave way to others, from the Babylonians to the Persians. The Sumerians adored making lists and counting things, which led them to invent a writing system called cuneiform. Instead of using papyrus paper like the Egyptians, they wrote on small clay tablets.

CHAPTER 10

Deborah and Jael of Israel

(A C T I V E   A R O U N D   1 2 0 0 - 1 1 0 0   B . C .)

There were no soft and fluffy "Debbies" 3,200 years ago. The first famous Deborah in history was tough as nails; she had to be, to become a leader and prophet of Israel. She lived in an age when the idea of women having power—to say nothing of brains—met with a "huh?" from most male Israelites in the loosely knit group of twelve Jewish tribes.

Just before Deborah's day, the Israelites had come out of Egypt, crossed the Jordan River, and moved back into what was then called Canaan. The place was already pretty full; its tribes of Canaanites and other -ites weren't happy to see more settlers. Nevertheless, the Israelites elbowed in, determined to make a home in this place where God had said the children of Israel belonged. It wasn't easy, learning to be farmers after they had lived as nomads. Other tribes attacked them again and again. The Canaanites, who were especially powerful, had been pounding on the Israelites for twenty years before Deborah was born.

She grew up in the beautiful hill country around Mount Ephraim, south of the main Canaanite stronghold. Although the Old Testament says nothing of her life as a girl, she no doubt passed her days as other girls did. She dressed in a long woolen garment called a simlah, trimmed on four corners with tassels the color of blue hyacinths. On feast days, she would have worn her best gold necklace or ring, or perhaps a nose jewel. She also had a heavier wrap; it served as a coat when it was cold, a blanket when she slept, and as a handy place to stash the unbaked loaves of bread she made each day and carried to the community oven.

When she married Lappidoth, a man who made candles for religious rites, Deborah wore traditional bridal finery. Afterwards, as a newly married woman, she covered her hair with a shawl whenever she went outside.

Even as a young wife, Deborah must have been very wise, judging by the number of men and women who went to her for sensible good advice. Her "office" was a shady seat beneath a palm tree in front of her house. There, somewhere on the road between the villages of Beth-el and Ramah, Deborah helped to solve problems. She answered religious questions, acted as a counseler in

THE LOST TRIBES OF ISRAEL

In Deborah's time, "the children of Israel" were organized into twelve tribes or clans. Much later, the Jews were conquered and spent years of exile in faraway Babylon. Not all of them returned to the Holy Land. People still claim that some of the "lost tribes of Israel" ended up on other continents, and evolved into other nations.

family quarrels, and as a judge for property disputes. Deborah also had psychic gifts. As a clairvoyant and prophet, she looked into the future and gave people advice about their life choices.

Because of her work and her far-seeing judgment, Deborah's name was already a household word among the Israelites when the trouble brewing with their traditional enemy, the Canaanites, came to a full boil. Their enemy had developed a scary new technology: iron chariots. Sisera, the Canaanite general, led a fast, highly mobile army of horsemen, foot soldiers, and warriors fighting from chariots—nine hundred of them. This was especially devastating to low-tech foot soldiers like the Israelites.

In their last battle, the Canaanites had badly beaten the Israelites. The losers had to pay the Canaanites tribute—a sort of loser's tax. The next time, it could be even worse: the Israelites might be pushed from their new homeland. The time had come for a major showdown.

On her own initiative, Deborah came forward. As she later wrote in her "memoirs" (set to music and sung for centuries), "Champions there were none, none left in Israel, until I, Deborah, arose, a mother in Israel." Her first job was to find a competent army commander. She'd heard good things about a seasoned soldier named Barak, who lived well to the north of her. So she sent for him.

"I want you to recruit 10,000 men from the Naphtali and Zebulun tribes in your area. I've got a military strategy that will work. We're going to fight the Canaanites—and win for a change. God has spoken to me," Deborah said.

Barak, who knew Deborah by reputation and respected her, consented on one condition. "This will only work if you come with me," he said.

"Of course I will," said Deborah. "That's the prophesy I received—that God will deliver the enemy general into the hands of a woman."

Together, they went north to the city of Kedesh and got commitments for the best young fighting men from the Israelite tribes. Even though some of the twelve tribes refused to take part, they soon had the ten thousand troops Deborah had asked for.

Deborah and Barak assembled their forces on the hillside of Mount Tabor, overlooking the city of Tanaach and the great river

valley of Jezreel, the scene of many past conflicts. By now, the thunder of Canaanite horses and chariots and the noise of thousands of men gathering in the valley below made General Barak and the outnumbered Israelite troops nervous and afraid. The opposing general deliberately pitched his tent close by, raising the fear level among the Israelites even higher. Deborah calmed Barak, and then went over her battle plan with him.

"I'm going to lure the enemy chariots west, toward the Kishon River," she said. "Once I've drawn Sisera and his main forces close to the water, I want to you attack from Mount Tabor, and crunch the Canaanites between us."

Barak watched as the first part of Deborah's plan unfolded. Then, as he and the Israelites began the charge down the slopes of Mount Tabor, God delivered on schedule. A mighty storm broke at their backs, sending rain and hail into the Canaanites' faces, ruining the aim of their archers, and spooking the horses pulling the iron chariots. The rains quickly turned the Kishon River into a huge lake of mud and swift currents. Canaanites and chariots alike floundered and went under. With their arrows and swords flashing, the Israelites gleefully tore the enemy army to shreds. It was payback time.

In the bloody confusion and blinding rain, no one spotted the once-cocky General Sisera jump from his chariot and run from the scene on foot.

Hours later, wet and exhausted, he reached his destination: the tent of a nomadic ally named Heber, a longtime Canaanite sympathizer who lived with his wife and a few goats. A place of refuge, Sisera thought. He would regroup, report to his king, and go whip the Israelites another day. He'd done it before.

Heber wasn't home, but his wife Jael greeted the general in a friendly fashion, then brought him something to eat and drink in her best dishes.

Feeling more in charge, the general said, "Now, I want you to guard the tent entrance while I catch a few winks. Don't let anyone know I'm here!"

Jael must have smiled a very special smile at that moment. "Oh, I won't let anyone see you in this tent," she promised. Sisera, confident he'd gotten out of the enemy's clutches, pulled up a cover and went to sleep.

Jael waited until the general made the regular sounds of deep slumber. Then she quietly picked up an iron tent stake and a hammer, crept to Sisera's side, and drove her weapon through the general's skull and pinned it to the ground. (Why a tent stake, you might ask? The holy scriptures said that women were forbidden to handle conventional weapons like swords—so resourceful Jael used what was handy!)

Before dusk, Barak showed up, following Sisera's trail. Jael came out to meet him, saying, "I've got the man you're looking for." When he entered the tent, Barak got a shock. There was his dead rival, dispatched in a way as brutal as death on the battlefield. At that moment, Barak saw that Deborah's prediction had a double meaning.

Two daring women, probably unknown to each other but linked in a mysterious way, had saved the young nation of Israel: Deborah, who led an army to victory; and Jael, who rid their world of an enemy leader. Even though not all the Israelite tribes participated, this was Israel's first national war of liberation. The Canaanites never attacked them again. If the account of Josephus (a Jewish historian of later times) is correct, Deborah herself lived a long life. She and General Barak gave their nation forty years of peace.

What's more, they gave their people a hit song! A pretty fair poet as well as a prophet, Deborah wrote a 31-verse creation called

"The Song of Deborah and Barak." It was meant to be sung to harp music—most poetry was back then. Written somewhere around 1125 before the common era, it survives to our day as the longest verse in the Old Testament, Chapter Five in the Book of Judges. In it, Deborah gave full credit to the actions of her long-distance ally Jael, calling her "blessed above women."

Thirty-two centuries separate the lives of Deborah and Golda Meir, the world-famous Prime Minister of Israel who led her country from 1969 to 1973. Yet these women had much in common. Both had that rare combination of wisdom, lion-hearted courage, and compassion for others—the definition of a great leader.

FOLLOWING IN DEBORAH'S FOOTSTEPS

Israel's history includes three women leaders as outstanding as any men: Deborah in the twelfth century before the common era, Queen Salome Alexandra in the first century before the common era, and Golda Meir in the twentieth century. Queen Salome (not the dirty dancing Salome!) Alexandra ruled as a widow. She stopped the constant warfare her husband had pursued, reversed his unfriendly policies toward the Pharisees, and gave her land eleven years of peace. Golda Meir helped in the birth of the modern state of Israel. Born in Russia, raised in the United States, she went to Palestine in 1921, first working on a kibbutz or communal farm to make the desert bloom. Then she entered politics, spent years fund-raising for Israel, and eventually became Prime Minister, guiding her country through war and peace.

CHAPTER 11

Zenobia of Palmyra

(ACTIVE 269 A.D.)

Heroic women were meat and drink to Zenobia, the wild-cat warrior queen of the Syrian desert. She grew up on stories about Queen Semiramis of Assyria; Elissa, the Phoenician founder of Carthage; and the dynasty of royal Cleopatras. When she grew older, Zenobia even claimed to have the Macedonian Greek blood of the Cleopatras in her veins. That was quite possible; her family tree had Greek, Roman, Arab, Bedouin, and Jewish branches, the same mix of cultures found in her home city of Palmyra.

Born about 241 A.D., she was named for, and resembled, her mother. They were both called al-Zabba, the local dialect for "the one with the long, lovely hair." (Only later did she become more famous as Septimia Zenobia, the Latin version of her name.) Mother and daughter had the classic beauty admired by the desert poets: huge dark eyes, perfect teeth, and flawless skin. She and her mother must have been close. Even on official documents, Zenobia often identified herself in a way that also honored her mother—as Bat Zabbai, or "daughter of al-Zabba."

Everyone in cosmopolitan Palmyra, not just Zenobia, knew several languages. As the wealthy daughter of a general, Zenobia studied languages as well as philosophy, history, and other subjects considered appropriate for a well-educated girl. Besides the local tongue, a mix of Aramaic (also used by Jesus, 250 years earlier) and Syrian Arabic, she became fluent in Greek and Egyptian.

Although Rome was Palmyra's political master, it seemed a million miles away. In the clear desert air, Zenobia must have loved to listen to the hubbub of the marketplace, and to watch the exchange of goods at this crossroads of the world: the finest silks, perfume in alabaster jars, ebony from Africa, jade from China, ivory from India, and swords from Italy.

In this long-ago time and place, girls matured early. When Zenobia grew to be a teen, Odenathus, the middle-aged ruler of

PALMYRA, BRIDE OF THE DESERT

Originally a village called Tadmor, Palmyra in the third century A.D. had grown into an important and rich Roman city, nicknamed "the bride of the desert." It sat where the main trade routes crossed, its caravans coming from Babylon and Persia to the east, Damascus and Jerusalem and Egypt to the south and west. As the camel drivers said, Palmyra was better than a mirage. After travelers plodded through hundreds of miles of burning desert, Palmyra suddenly appeared, an exquisite oasis, greenly shaded by great palm trees, its noble palaces and parks shimmering in the Syrian sand, the whole city mirrored in a shallow salt lake to the east.

Palmyra, happened to be looking for a new wife. This thirty-something military commander already had a son about Zenobia's age from a previous marriage. Odenathus and Zenobia married when she was about fourteen—the typical age for brides back then.

Odenathus had a lot to offer. He was at the peak of his power. The Romans were grateful to the Palmyrenes and their splendid army of archers for beating the Persians in battle—and for keeping Persians out of the not-so-mighty-anymore Roman Empire. They'd given the city many privileges. Palmyra got to resell the luxury goods that poured into the city from all directions. Better yet, the city collected taxes on everything—and didn't have to pay tribute to Rome. The Romans gave Odenathus a variety of titles, too. In addition to Palmyra and its 150,000 inhabitants, he ruled a much larger area of Syrian desert, studded with smaller oasis settlements called Palmyrena.

Despite their age difference, Odenathus and Zenobia had interests in common. Both loved to ride and hunt. Together, they would ride into the desert and the hills north and east of the city, returning with gazelle, wild boar, and even lions—the most exciting and worthy trophies a hunter could win.

During her years of marriage, Zenobia only slowed down her active life to bear two sons, or possibly three. The oldest boy, Wahballath, was born around 256 A.D.

About ten years after Wahballath's birth, King Odenathus and his grown son Herodes were returning to Palmyra from a war victory. They stopped at Emesa for a Syrian cousin's birthday party. Instead of cake and ice cream, they got murdered. When she received the shocking news, Zenobia speedily brought the conspirators to trial and had them executed. Despite her actions, there were always ill-natured rumors that the queen herself had had some hand in the deaths.

One thing is certain: Zenobia, who now ruled Palmyra for her 10-year-old son, Wahballath, loved being in charge. She brought together a group of brilliant scholars and philosophers from Greece and elsewhere for her court. She began to issue coins with her image on them. At her splendid palace, dressed in brocaded silks, she served wine from a collection of gold goblets that were said to have belonged to Cleopatra the Seventh, Egypt's most famous queen. Whenever Zenobia appeared in public or led her troops, she wore a helmet that caught every eye. From it hung a great glowing jewel the color of amethyst.

Palmyra was rich and prosperous enough that Zenobia could have done little and lived in luxury. But she was a risk-taker, a gambler in the same mold as the female rulers she admired. Queen Zenobia wanted to make Palmyra a world power. And she had good reasons for believing it was possible. First, she and her husband had kept the neighboring empire of Persia from spreading west. As a result, Rome treated Palmyra as a political equal instead of as just another foreign state belonging to the Roman Empire. Second, she saw that the Roman Empire had grown flabby, its leaders weak.

To realize her ambition, Queen Zenobia first grabbed the rest of Syria and Palestine. Then she marched her army of archers and cavalry units into Egypt for another victory. Soon, her general reported back that the lands as far north as Ankara (a city in today's Turkey) were hers.

Zenobia's actions took a while to sink in with the Romans, who were busy fighting the Goths in northern Italy. By the time they did, this can-do woman had cut off the vital wheat supplies that fed Rome from the world's breadbasket, Egypt. The Romans were outraged. A client state that was supposed to belong to Rome—one run by a female to boot—had gained control of the eastern third of what was supposed to be the Roman Empire!

In 270 A.D., the newly proclaimed Roman Emperor Aurelian hurried to the Near East to confront her. Aurelian had no experience as an emperor; unluckily for Zenobia, however, he was one of Rome's best generals.

Giovanni Battista Tiepolo, *Queen Zenobia Addressing Her Soldiers*, Samuel H. Kress Collection, ©1997 Board of Trustees, National Gallery of Art, Washington.

The two armies clashed near Antioch, and again at Emesa. After two huge and hard-fought battles, Aurelian finally beat Zenobia's larger forces. Now in retreat, Zenobia started preparing her city of Palmyra for a siege. Then her Armenian allies deserted. In a desperate move, Zenobia made a last-minute run for the Persian border to plead for reinforcements, only to be intercepted by the Romans and taken prisoner. Hearing the news, her city surrendered.

Aurelian thought of Zenobia as a very worthy opponent. There was little bloodshed. After being taken prisoner, however, she and her sons were dragged around the countryside with the Roman army for nearly a year while Aurelian mopped up the remains of her rebellion, which flared up again in Egypt and in Palmyra.

In 273 A.D., the people of Rome gathered to gawk at one of the most extravagant spectacles a returning emperor or general had ever given. The parade (called a triumph) began with twenty elephants, four tigers, giraffes, and other wild beasts. These curiosities were followed by 800 pairs of gladiators and hundreds of captives, each person identified by place of origin with a sign. The triumph even included a group of ten female warriors who'd fought with the Goths. Their labels read "Amazon." Finally came the wonder everyone had been talking about—rebellious Zenobia, on foot in front of her own glittering chariot, her chin high, wearing her best jewels and manacled with so many chains of gold on her hands, feet, and neck that the weight had to be partly carried by the Persian jester at her side.

Instead of the savage treatment other daring women sometimes got, Zenobia survived. As a mark of respect, Aurelian granted her a pension and a place to live near Tivoli, a 750-acre fantasy park of architecture and landscaping that echoed the wonders of the Roman Empire. What did Zenobia think about as she wandered through its temples, villas, and rose gardens? Perhaps she recalled her ravaged city of Palmyra, and the famous saying about Roman military tactics that still offers a message to warring nations today: "They make a desert, and call it peace."

Aurelian himself was murdered one year after his triumph. It's said that Zenobia married again—to a Roman senator this time. A century after this wily woman made international news, her descendants could still be counted among the nobles of Rome.

CHAPTER 12

Enheduana of Sumer

(ACTIVE 2300 B.C.)

You might call Enheduana one of history's first bookworms. Perhaps she brought books to the dinner table. If so, they looked like small clay pillows, not paperbacks. In her day, almost 4,300 years ago, "books" were written on soft clay with a pointed tool called a stylus. It was a big deal, learning to read back then. Enheduana not only read well, she wrote well. In fact, she became the world's first bestselling author as well as the most famous poet from the ancient land of Sumer.

Enheduana, her twin brothers Rimush and Manishtusu, and her father Sargon lived in a spanking-new big palace, surrounded by the city-state of Akkad in Sumer (located about where Baghdad is today). King Sargon, an ambitious boy from a family of Mesopotamian farmers, began his rise to the top as a humble cupbearer for the king of Kish, a nearby city-state. No one knows how he managed to grab the throne for himself, but he did. Soon he expanded his rule over Kish and Akkad and made them important cities of Sumer, a flat and fertile crescent of land between two great rivers in what is now Iraq. (In Enheduana's day, "countries" as we know them didn't really exist yet—instead, independent cities like Akkad, Kish, and Ur fought to control larger regions of land. Political power and political boundaries changed hands all the time.)

NOT-SO-GOLDEN SCHOOL DAYS

Most boys in ancient Mesopotamia went to school, called an "edubba" or "tablet house" after the clay tablets everyone wrote on. Besides mastering the cuneiform writing with its 500 basic signs, students learned math, geometry, and grammar. Very few girls attended edubba, however. School was a lot tougher then. Besides holding class from dawn to dusk, teachers thought that knowledge needed to be pounded in, so pupils got whippings almost every day! Girls were most likely taught at home or by tutors. Despite the obstacles, enough girls learned to read and write so that gradually a new written dialect just for women, called Emesal, came into being. It used word endings and vocabulary that were different from the standard language. It must have been a great way for women to send secret messages! Archaeologists also find Emesal very handy when trying to figure out who wrote a given document. For instance, they discovered several tablets that contained a long, name-calling argument, evidently between two people. The authors' names, however, were missing. Because this literary "catfight" was in the distinctive Emesal dialect, they know it must have been written by two educated—and, by the sound of it, very angry!—women.

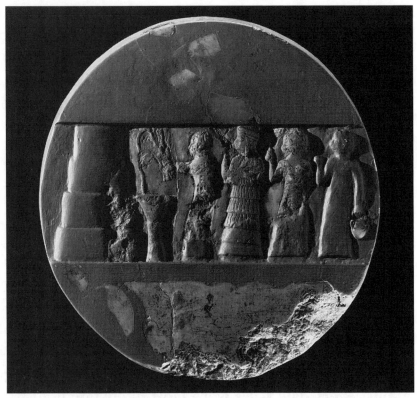

University of Pennsylvania Museum, Philadelphia (Neg # S4-139330)

Naturally, Sargon expected Enheduana's kid brothers to follow in his footsteps as kings of Sumer and Akkad one day. Unfortunately, the twins had the yen to be kings, but not the talent.

Enheduana, on the other hand, soon showed that she had talent and drive to spare. When she became a teenager, her dad thought she was ready for grownup responsibility. He appointed her to be the high priestess to Nanna, the important moon-god of Sumer.

To perform her duties as high priestess, Enheduana had to leave her hometown of Akkad and move south to Ur, one of the most sacred cities in Sumer. Ur sat near the Persian Gulf, its houses and buildings clustered around a tall ziggurat, a temple that looked like a pyramid with steps. Each of the ziggurat's seven stories was painted a different color. The top story was painted blue. Enheduana used the room at the very top, nearest the heavens.

Enheduana's people believed in many gods and goddesses. Only through the priestess's hard work would the higher powers smile on the land and keep the crops, animals, and people well and prosperous. Wearing her special cap, carrying a mace, and dressed in a long embroidered gown with rows of ruffles, Enheduana offered prayers and carried out rituals throughout the year. On the altars at the top of the ziggurat, she made animal sacrifices. To please the gods and goddesses, she also burned incense and other perfumed resins, sending the sweet-smelling smoke through the clear blue skies of Sumer. (Our word "perfume" actually means "through smoke.")

Her most important ritual duty was the annual New Year celebration each spring. (Early religions often celebrated the new year in the spring because people wanted to encourage the growth of crops.) The ceremony retold the story of a sacred marriage between a shepherd named Dumuzi and the moon-goddess Inanna. Inside her blue room high in the ziggurat, Enheduana as the goddess-bride and one of the reigning kings or high priests would reenact the marriage of a goddess and a human each year, to keep the gods happy.

Besides her spiritual duties as high priestess, a position she kept for nearly twenty-five years, Enheduana channeled much of her religious feeling into her writing. She wrote a set of forty-two poems or hymns to the temples of Sumer and Akkad. Although a priestess of the moon-god originally, Enheduana began to identify more with the moon-goddess Inanna. She wrote a great cycle of poetry to her, which was probably sung and performed, called the Exaltation of Inanna. Thanks to her influence, Inanna (later called Ishtar) gradually became the supreme being in the land of Sumer.

Enheduana's poems were very popular in her day and long after. Because she wrote on clay tablets, which were much more durable than paper, archaeologists have found over fifty tablets with the same poem on them. For Enheduana's time, this was like going platinum or making the bestseller list.

Enheduana's writings tell us much about herself, the Sumerian religion, and even politics. For instance, she wrote an exciting account about her father. At one point, the city-states that Sargon had taken united in revolt against him. They besieged the city of Akkad and exiled the goddess Inanna from her temples. Sargon finally broke the siege, beat the rebels, and made them recognize the goddess Inanna as all-powerful.

Enheduana kept on composing poetry and taking care of her religious responsibilities, even after her father died. Her brother Rimush, the older twin, ruled first. Then Manishtusu (named "who is with him?" by the surprised midwife who delivered the babies) took over. Both brothers loved bloodshed; both were killed in turn by palace enemies who hated them. Then a nephew of Enheduana's came into power. In spite of her long experience, popularity, and royal background, Enheduana lost her priestess post. Her nephew kicked her out, possibly exiling her to the desert. Then he installed his own daughter as high priestess.

But Enheduana ended up having the last laugh. And the last word, literally. No one remembers her nasty nephew King Naram-

Sin today. Enheduana, however, has become a famous first: she is the very earliest author, male or female, to be known by name. Her poems, written around 2300 B.C., are the first creations anywhere in the world credited to an individual person. A verse from one of them shows her spirit:

The first lady of the throne room
has accepted Enheduana's song.
Inanna loves her again.
The day was good for Enheduana, for she was
        dressed in jewels.
She was dressed in womanly beauty.
Like the moon's first rays over the horizon,
how luxuriously she was dressed!
When Nanna, Inanna's father, made his entrance
the palace blessed Inanna's mother Ningal.
From the doorsill of heaven came the word: "Welcome!"

There is a proverb from Enheduana's day, written in a dialect used by women only, called Emesal. It says: "My mouth makes me comparable with men." That proud statement, written by an unknown woman, could have come from the smiling lips of Enheduana herself.

CHAPTER 13

Semiramis of Assyria

(A C T I V E   8 0 0   B . C .)

Halfway through his 334 to 323 B.C. conquer-the-world tour, Alexander the Great came across a huge message carved into the side of a cliff. After he read it, he knew that another world conqueror had already "been there, done that" five hundred years earlier. Her name was Queen Semiramis.

Semiramis was a true Assyrian leader. She didn't believe in being modest. Carved boldly into the side of the cliff were her words: "I ruled the empire of Ninus, which reaches eastward to the river Indus, southward to the land of incense and myrrh, northward to the Saces and Sogdians. Before me, no Assyrian had ever seen a sea—I have seen four which none have approached, so far away are they. I compelled rivers to run where I wished and directed their courses to places where they were needed. I watered the barren lands with my rivers. I built up impregnable fortresses. With iron tools, I made roads across impassable rock. I opened them for my chariots in places where even wild beasts had not been able to pass. Yet in the midst of all these occupations, I found time for pleasure, I found time for love."

The inscription Alex admired was one of many this queen of Assyria put up. In days of old, this was a favorite royal hobby. Inscriptions carved in stone were permanent billboards, which rulers used to brag about their deeds so no one would forget them. Sometimes their boasts were full of hype. In the case of Semiramis, however, archaeologists continue to find evidence to prove some of her claims. For instance, they've found markers showing that she reached India to the east, Turkey to the west, and the Arabian peninsula to the south—an incredible 1600 miles from her central city of Babylon.

Because Semiramis' deeds were as flashy as her self-promotion, Greek historians raved about her exploits for centuries. Sometimes their reports made her into a Wonder Woman who conquered fabled lands like Ethiopia. They said she fought a huge army in India, fooling her opponents by putting thousands of fake elephants (decoys made from cattle hides) at the head of her army. Greek writers even transformed her into a goddess. At the end of her human life, they claimed, Semiramis turned herself into a dove and flew away to heaven.

What was the down-to-earth Semiramis like? For starters, she wasn't born an Assyrian. She came from the royal family of Chaldea, a region south of Babylon between the Euphrates River and the Persian Gulf. Marrying a Chaldean princess seemed like a good move politically for King Shamsi-Adad of neighboring Assyria. A few years after they were married, an event the king longed for came to pass: Semiramis had a baby boy, Adad-Nirari, who would inherit the throne someday.

About 811 B.C., however, the king died in a military campaign. The queen didn't spend much time moping, however; her capital city and the surrounding country were a real mess. A revolt within the city of Babylon, which her husband had put down with much destruction and bloodshed, had left the skyline of the city flatter than a cheese pizza. Now ruling for her son, Queen Semiramis set out to make Babylon bigger and more beautiful than before.

First the queen built a thirty-foot-wide stone and cedar bridge across the Euphrates River, which divided the city in two. At either end, she put up palaces, their enameled brick walls alive with wild animals in vivid colors. In the larger palace, which faced the setting sun, the walls shimmered with a huge mural of Semiramis on horseback, throwing a javelin at a leopard. (Centuries later, researchers made a thrilling discovery in the ruins. After looking through millions of broken bricks, they unearthed a tiny piece of tile with the white face of a woman on it—the only human image ever found there.)

Semiramis loved big engineering projects. Over the years, she built roads nonstop, such as the one from Ecbatana (Hamadan in

NO BAD HAIR DAYS IN OLD ASSYRIA

Even though she plastered her name all over Assyria, no clearly identified portraits of Semiramis have been found. It's a pretty safe bet she was obsessed with her hair—all Assyrians were. Men and women alike wore their hair long and elaborately cut, layered, styled, oiled, and curled. Every day, servants would crimp and curl Semiramis' hair. Braiding was very popular; so were corn-rows along the sides and tight curls glued to the forehead with perfumed gel. (The men even wore spit curls in their beards!) Once, Semiramis was in the middle of a comb-out, getting her dark locks arranged into a beautifully braided do, when someone rushed in to say that fighting had broken out in Babylon. Immediately the queen became all business. She jumped up, grabbed her weapons and armor, and led her forces with half of her hair sticking out all over the place. To prove she was serious, she didn't let anyone finish styling her hair until the rebellion had been put down. The Assyrians were so impressed with her devotion that they put up a large statue of Semiramis, pictured with her hair braided on one side, flowing loose on the other. That statue reminded everyone what a strong-minded person this Assyrian fireball was.

today's Iran) into the savage Zagros Mountains that form the Iran-Iraq border. She turned the towns of Nimrod and Nineveh into imposing cities of 100,000 people. She was fascinated by irrigation problems. To make her dry farmlands capable of feeding a growing population, she built a huge new network of canals to water the rich soil between the Tigris and Euphrates rivers.

Once she ordered her crews to go into the distant mountains of Armenia, quarry out a massive piece of stone, haul it with oxen and mule teams on logs to the river, load it onto a giant raft, and bring it downstream to the city of Babylon. When the weary men finally got the giant chunk of stone to the city, Semiramis ordered it to be carved into an obelisk shape (like the Washington Monument) and set up on the busiest street of Babylon. Even in a city filled with ziggurat temples, palaces, and high walls, her monument stood out. It pierced the bright blue sky, reaching as high as a 14-story apartment building, some 135 feet tall and about 25 feet square.

BUILDING A LEGEND AROUND SEMIRAMIS

Our eager builder queen got credited with countless architectural achievements. For instance, she was often called the brains behind the Hanging Gardens of Babylon, one of the seven ancient wonders of the world. (It *was* built for a woman—a queen who lived three hundred years after Semiramis.) Archaeologists are still looking for evidence to prove other deeds that the ancient writers called hers. One of the most interesting was a brick-lined, tar-coated tunnel that provided a secure, all-weather walkway under the Euphrates river and connected the two riverbank palaces of Semiramis.

A MILITARY SECRET BECOMES A FASHION FIRST

This inventive queen was also credited with a contribution that means a whole lot in our modern world: the invention of trousers. According to Greek historian Diodorus, when Semiramis was about to set off on a long and difficult journey, she dreamed up the pants notion. Her first priority? Camouflage. As a military leader, she wanted to make it hard to tell if the horseback rider was a man or a woman. Semiramis also wanted a pliable garment that protected her skin, kept her warm, and was comfortable. Her forerunners to our blue jeans were so pleasant to wear that their use eventually spread to Persia, Syria, and other countries in the Near East.

It's clear Semiramis wanted to be remembered for a long time. But she also worked hard to leave a stronger country for her son Adad-Nirari. Until the boy was about 18, she ruled Assyria and spent an amazing amount of time leading an army. Like the macho Assyrian kings who preceded her, she loved a good military campaign, and tried to explore and conquer everything in sight.

Once her son Adad-Nirari became king of Assyria, his mother took a backseat in public life. When Semiramis died, however, her son proudly put up one last monument to this great queen. In the ancient capital of Ashur, he placed her carved stele (stone pillar) among the pillars of the other rulers of Assyria, where archaeologists found it, still standing, in this century.

BORROWING A FEW TRICKS FROM A LEGEND

Nearly three thousand years after Semiramis romped around Mesopotamia, an English archaeologist named Sir Austen Henry Layard used her know-how to solve a big problem. In the 1890s—Layard's day—no visible signs of the powerful nation of Assyria remained standing in Iraq. He, however, had dug up a series of massive statues at the buried city of Nimrod and wanted to move them. Layard was stumped; local people no longer remembered how to do such things. So Layard studied Queen Semiramis' method of moving great masses of stone, and copied her. He had simple rolling platforms made from tree trunks, put the statues on the platforms, and had teams of animals pull them to the Tigris River. From there, the heavy sculptures were floated downstream on rafts. Thanks to the engineering clues left by Semiramis, the entrance to the Assyrian exhibit at the British Museum in London is now guarded by these amazing figures. With the bodies of bulls, human heads, and great wings, the statues loom fourteen feet high.

Village people throughout Mesopotamia, the land between two rivers, have remembered Semiramis in their own fashion. Ever since her time, locals refer to every single one of the ruined cities, walls, burial mounds, and ancient towers that dot their land as "the works of Semiramis."

V

GREEN VILLAGES, GREAT WALLS

The Far East

ONE OF THE MOST *beloved flowers in Asia is the lily, seen in paintings, on jade carvings, and on porcelain vases everywhere. With its air of permanence and its ability to spread and multiply, the lily could stand for early Asian cultures also. Early in its history, China's immense plains and river valleys became one country culturally. No wonder that its literature, art, and medicine are so highly developed—the Chinese have been working on them for 4,000 years. Always a land of serious thinkers and seekers, China was the birthplace of Confucianism and Taoism. Here too an early system of writing developed, and so did building projects such as the Great Wall. Like a vigorous lily plant, China's influence eventually spread to Vietnam and other Asian neighbors. Over the centuries, this crossing of cultures has given each country in southeast Asia its own special flavor.*

CHAPTER 14

Pan Chao of China

(ACTIVE 90 A.D.)

As a little girl, Pan Chao loved to hear her older brothers Ku and Ch'ao tell the family stories. Her favorite was the one about the family's most honored ancestor, who had been abandoned in a swamp, brought up by tigers, and later given the name Ku-Wu-T'u, or "milk of the tiger." Chao loved the fact that her family name, Pan, was another word for tiger.

Although she obeyed her father as a good daughter from a Chinese noble family should, Chao was as fierce as her tiger ancestor about one thing: education. Once she tasted the delights of knowledge, she wouldn't let go. Luckily, her parents agreed. Since girls didn't get to attend formal school in her day, both her parents and her brothers took turns teaching Chao at home.

Scholarship was in her blood. Originally the family had lived near the Great Wall of China. After they became wealthy from cattle and sheep ranching, the Pan family eagerly turned to pursuits of the mind. Chao's great-grandfather was so clever

that he was invited to the royal court at Changan, China's first capital city.

Chao was born in Changan and lived there with her parents and twin brothers. Like the Great Wall further north, Chao's home city had huge walls thirty feet high, curling around the city like a stone dragon. Later called Sian, Changan was the center of the Chinese empire, the place where all the trade routes crossed. Around the city grew immense fields of wheat and cotton.

Her father, who was writing a lengthy history of the Han dynasty, often told her, "You are fortunate to live in peaceful times." When he was younger, he had suffered through a political coup—the only break in nearly 400 years of peace.

The governing powers, known as the great Han dynasty, made the first century A.D. a golden age. Families prospered. More children got an education (though most of them were boys). Safe roads made travel easier, and traders brought exotic goods from faraway places like India and England.

An eager reader from an early age, Chao soon followed her own interests in literature, astronomy, and mathematics. She spent a lot of time in her home's library. There, in the place of honor, sat the rare books given to the family by an earlier emperor. Her father used them as a resource for his own historical research. Chao's mother was fond of the literary classics. She made sure that her bookish daughter got training in poetry and literature, as well as in good manners and eloquence.

Before Chao's tenth birthday, a great sadness hit the household. Her father died, his book on the history of the Han dynasty still unfinished. Her brother Ku, the more studious of the twins, vowed to complete the book. Chao wanted to help him, but she

LIVING IN HAN DYNASTY TIMES

During its four hundred years, the Han dynasty of emperors gave the country unity and peace. The emperors presided over great achievements in medicine, science, the arts, and religion. The use of paper for writing—and for paper money—came into being. So did the first attempts at earthquake prediction. Buddhism was introduced. There was intense interest in alchemy and the search for a way to turn metals into gold—an activity that was being paralleled around the Mediterranean by European alchemists.

was too young. And she was a female in a Confucian society, where only males had status.

Chao's main duty was to marry. When she was fourteen, no matter what her own desires were, she became the bride of a man named Ts'ao Shih-shu, from a neighboring clan. Soon they began a family. After some twenty years of marriage, Shih-shu died, leaving Chao a widow in her thirties with three grown children. Ordinarily, Chao would remain with her husband's family, under the thumb of her mother-in-law, as custom demanded. But Chao bucked tradition and did an extraordinary thing. She returned to her family home, now in the new capital of Lo-Yang. There she settled in with her mother and her older brother Ku, who was still sweating over that bulky history begun by Chao's dad so many years before.

A couple of years later, in 92 A.D., Chao's son won a job at a city three hundred miles east of Lo-Yang. He invited her to come along and to live with him. Her journey set off a creative urge.

BOUND TO OBEY

In China, Confucianism (developed by the sage Confucius) was an ethical way of life rather than a religion. Although it had many good points, Confucianism oppressed women. From childhood, a woman practiced the Three Obediences: first to her father, next to her husband, and then (if her husband died before she did) to her oldest son. Under Confucianism, peasant women had an easier time of it than did upper-class women. This was especially true from the tenth century on, when the feet of noble women were cruelly bound into tiny "golden lilies," a deformity that left them unable to walk.

Chao began to pour out her feelings, and wrote a long poem called "Traveling Eastward." In it, she wrote, "Secretly I sigh for the capital city I love, but to cling to one's native place characterizes a small nature, as the histories have taught us."

While she was with her son in Lo-Yang, two other events changed Chao's life. Her brother Ku died, the great book still unfinished. And Emperor Ho, who'd heard many times from her brother that Chao was also a fine historian, sent word that he wanted Chao to finish it! With joy she went to live in the royal court, working nonstop at the Tung Kuan library until she had the pleasure of telling the emperor, "The history—all 31 volumes—is complete!" She did much more than edit and complete a chapter or two. Chao wrote over 25 percent of the book, including the section on astronomy.

Because Chao was so good at history and other subjects, she became the unofficial historian of China—at that time one of the most powerful empires in the world. She was also named poet laureate, chief poet of the land. Pleased with her work, Emperor Ho then asked her to tutor his new empress, 15-year-old Teng. For ten years, Chao worked with the empress and became a valued friend as well as mentor. As a sign of respect, the empress and the rest of the court began to call Chao "Ta ku—Honored Aunt."

After Ho died, Empress Teng began to rule as regent for her small son, often asking for her teacher's advice on political matters. Chao preferred the contemplative life of books, research, and philosophy, but she was a realist. She knew the energetic empress valued her common sense, so she stayed on at court and conferred with the empress often.

Chao was extra-busy with other projects too. Under her

supervision, a group of ten select historians did research. Somehow, Chao also found time to write sixteen books, from narrative poems to books of essays. She lived during an exciting period in China, when a new substance called "paper" was replacing silk and bamboo as writing material. In fact, some of the very first Chinese books written in calligraphy on paper may have been those of Pan Chao.

Chao once read a book that really stayed with her. It was a collection of biographies of well-known women from China's past. When Chao became well-known, she was asked to edit and add to the same book, *The Biographies of Eminent Women*. That book, and her own experiences, made her put aside the Confucian modesty women were supposed to maintain and write her own book, called *Lessons for Women*. Even with her prestige, her book was considered outrageous. Why? Because she wanted more women to benefit from the education she had gotten.

In her book, she told people: "To teach men and not women—doesn't that ignore the essential relation between them? According to the rites, it's the rule to teach children to read at the age of eight, and by the age of fifteen they ought then to be ready for cultural training. Why shouldn't girls as well as boys be educated according to this principle?"

Interestingly, Pan Chao fought for female education—but not for female independence of movement or freedom of choice. Remember, she lived nineteen centuries ago, in a land where the idea of female equality remains a distant goal even today. Chao's courage did not change the great ebb and flow of events in China; but her words, like the glimpse of small bright birds on a gray day, left an indelible mark.

CHAPTER 15

Trung Trac and Trung Nhi of Vietnam

(ACTIVE ABOUT 39 A.D.)

At the very beginning of the first century A.D., two girls were born into a ruling family called Trung in northern Vietnam. Trac and her younger sister Nhi did everything together. Their home on a hill in Me Linh was pleasant. Their favorite playground, however, was the rich green delta of the Red River valley, an area bright with birds and swamp creatures. In their games, Trac always wanted to run things, solve puzzles, and boss her sister. Nhi, on the other hand, liked nothing better than to play warrior. People said that the sisters were very strong-minded. "Just like their father," some said. He was an important local ruler. "Just like their mother," others said. Although she busied herself with her family, Mrs. Trung had a quiet strength about her. She'd taught her daughters to be proud and independent.

By the time the Trung sisters were born, Vietnam had been under the thumb of Chinese rule for nearly two hundred years—

since 111 B.C. Once known in legend as Van Tang, "the country of the tattooed men," the Chinese now called the land Nam-Viet, "the people of the south."

Vietnamese culture gave women freedom to work, inherit, and be educated. Trac, who'd always had a way with words, grew into a woman with a commanding personality. Even after she married a local chief with substantial power, a fellow named Thi Sach, she and her sister remained tight friends.

About 39 A.D., the Chinese thought their Vietnamese subjects were acting far too much like free people. To teach them who was boss, To Dinh, the Chinese governor of Vietnam, decided to make a bloody example. He killed Trac's husband, who had openly criticized the Chinese. Just in case every single person hadn't

LIVING WITH A GIANT

Giant China was always peering over the shoulders of its neighbors, trying to rule them. Beginning in the second century B.C., the Chinese entered the land to the south, where tribal people they called "Nam-Viet" lived. Not all the changes made by Chinese rule were bad. The Chinese taught the Vietnamese how to cultivate rice in the fertile deltas to the north and south of the country. Because rice growing is a cooperative activity, the Vietnamese learned to pull together as a society. In the mountainous highlands of Vietnam, however, certain tribes retained their independence and cultures. Even today—and like its neighbors Thailand, Cambodia, and Laos—Vietnam still has many tribal groups with their own distinctive art, language, and customs.

gotten the message, To Dinh added a brutal encore. He assaulted Trung Trac, Sach's young widow.

Trac could have curled up and become a victim. Instead, she turned her grief and anger in another direction. With her sister's help, she rallied the Vietnamese community. To fight the Chinese, with all their resources, the sisters knew they would need good leadership. They set about training thirty-six candidates—most of them women—to lead. Trac and Nhi even talked their quiet clever mother into becoming a general!

It wasn't enough to have leaders. The Trung sisters needed followers—a lot of them. To win supporters, Trac and Nhi knew they had to show they had brains and courage.

"I've got an idea," said Trac to Nhi, or perhaps the other way around. "What about that tiger that's been attacking the villagers around Me Linh? Suppose we hunt it down. People will be grateful. And we'll show what we can do."

The sisters headed off into the lush Vietnamese countryside. When they finally succeeded in killing the animal, they tanned the tiger's beautiful skin. On the hide side, Trac and Nhi wrote a letter, asking everyone to join their fight against the Chinese oppressors. Beginning in the north, they took their persuasive "recruitment poster" to the cities and hamlets of Vietnam, displaying it everywhere.

In a short while, the sisters had pulled together an army of 80,000 peasants. They also got the promise of help from tribal leaders throughout the country.

With Trac planning the strategy, and younger sister Nhi leading the troops in battle, they drove vicious To Dinh, the Chinese

governor who'd been Vietnam's chief tyrant and Trac's attacker, out of the country. To Dinh had a close call. To escape the sisters after they attacked his home, he had to shave his head and beard, put on the saffron robe of a monk, and flee in disguise.

With the Trung sisters at the head of the army, sitting on matching elephants and waving their sabers, the Vietnamese freedom fighters won control of sixty-five towns. Eventually they claimed independence for an area that began at Hue, a city in the center of long slender Vietnam, and went all the way into southern China. To rub it in, Trac and Nhi set up a new capital at Me Linh (near today's capital, Hanoi), right in the faces of their opponents.

By popular acclaim, Trac, the older sister, was renamed Trung Vuong or "she-king Trung." For three years, these energetic sisters co-ruled the newly free Vietnamese, using their powers to push out the Chinese and get rid of the heavy taxes the Chinese had imposed. They worked hard, setting up a form of government more in harmony with their local traditions. They didn't forget defense, either. Everyone came to know The Citadel with Three Ponds, their headquarters in Me Linh, a fortress surrounded by walls eleven yards thick.

Eventually, however, the emperor of China got seriously mad. He sent huge numbers of troops into Vietnam to recapture it. Trac and Nhi still had highly motivated fighters like General Phung Thi Chinh, who led her soldiers even while she was pregnant—and, it was said, gave birth on the battlefield, then fought her way out with her newborn tied to her back and a sword in each hand. That might be a tall tale, but the Vietnamese commitment to freedom was not.

Even when the Chinese forces, through sheer numbers, finally turned the tables and beat the Vietnamese army, Trung Trac and Trung Nhi chose to leave this world as free people. A team until the last, the sisters committed ritual suicide by throwing themselves into the Day River, in the northern delta country of their birth.

The heroics of Trung Trac and Trung Nhi, their love of independence, and the example they left for other women, were never forgotten. Applauded in their lifetime, and venerated ever since, the sisters had temples built in their honor that still stand in Sontay, Hanoi, and other parts of Vietnam. Places like Hanoi's War Museum have permanent exhibits dedicated to the sisters. Each spring, on the sixth day of the second month, the Vietnamese people still gather to celebrate Trung Sisters day.

During the twentieth century, another Vietnamese leader believed she was the incarnation of the Trung sisters. Her name was Beautiful Spring, but the world came to know her as Madame Nhu, the notorious wife of the country's leader Diem. Although Madame Nhu put up a statue to the sisters, it was intended more as a monument for her own personal ambitions. Vietnam would have to wait a little longer for another pair of true patriots like Trung Trac and Trung Nhi to come along.

A LAND OF FEMALE FREEDOM FIGHTERS

Vietnam had more female heroes than the Trungs. One shining example was Trieu Thi Thrinh. Inspired by stories of the sisters, she followed their lead, and in 248 A.D. she roused the Vietnamese to push the Chinese out of their lands. By age 21, she'd led her people in thirty battles, and Vietnam was newly free. She too was defeated and took her own life rather than give herself up to the enemy. Trieu Thi Thrinh wanted freedom for women as much as freedom for her country. People still repeat the famous quote she made while arguing with her brother: "I will not resign myself to the usual lot of women who bow their heads and become concubines."

Note: Most of the primary sources used to write these biographies are difficult to read and understand, even for adults. A few noted below are excerpted in books suitable for motivated younger readers. For those who want to move to a more profound level of research, the Greek and Latin primary sources for the ancient world may be found in the Loeb Classical Library series (hardcover bilingual editions, published by Harvard University Press) and the Penguin Classics series (softcover, sometimes abridged editions, but easier to read). The asterisked items contain primary source material.

Ashby, Ruth, et al. *Herstory: Women Who Changed the World.* (Viking 1995).

Bianchi, Robert. *The Nubians, People of the Ancient Nile.* (Millbrook 1994).

Boccaccio, Giovanni. *Concerning Famous Women.* (Rutgers

University Press 1963). Written by a medieval "fan" of ancient women and riddled with errors, but a simply written book that clearly shows the ways in which women's history has been distorted.

Brooks, Polly S. *Cleopatra, Goddess of Egypt, Enemy of Rome*. (HarperCollins 1995).

Carter, Dorothy S. *His Majesty, Queen Hatshepsut*. (Lippincott 1987).

Chiera, Edward. *They Wrote on Clay*. (University of Chicago Press 1966). Excellent overview of cuneiform writing and the cultures of Mesopotamia.

Forbes, Malcolm. *Women Who Made a Difference*. (Simon & Schuster 1990). For young adult readers; contains some women from ancient times.

*Hirshfield, Jane, ed. *Women in Praise of the Sacred*. (HarperCollins 1994). Contains poems by Enheduana, Sappho, and others.

James, P. and Thorpe, N. *Ancient Inventions*. (Ballantine 1994). Recommended for understanding the underpinnings of the ancient world; easy to read.

León, Vicki. *Uppity Women of Ancient Times*. (Conari Press 1995). Brief biographies of 200 women between 2700 B.C. and 450 A.D.

Loeb Classical Library volumes of interest:

Greek Lyrics (5 volumes). Sappho and other Greek poets.

**Diogenes Laertius* (volume 2). Hipparchia and other philosophers.

**Select Papyri* (volumes 1 and 2). Wonderful letters, laundry lists, prayers, complaints, wills, etc., from ordinary people;

an excellent way to introduce the concept of primary source material to students.

National Geographic Society. *Everyday Life in Ancient Times*. (National Geographic Society 1958). Wonderful color renderings of life of the high and the humble in Mesopotamia, Egypt, ancient Greece, ancient Rome.

* Old Testament of the *Bible*. Book of Judges, Chapters 4 and 5, all verses. Notice how both chapters repeat the story of Deborah in different ways.

Slater, Elinor and Robert. *Great Jewish Women*. (Jonathan David 1994).

* Sweet, Waldo. *Sport and Recreation in Ancient Greece*. (Oxford University Press 1987). Excellent book of primary source excerpts for Hedea and other women in sports.

Wright, David. *Enchantment of the World, Vietnam*. (Childrens Press 1989).

T I M E L I N E

~~~~~~

(Most dates here and throughout the book are approximate.)

2300–2200 B.C.
Enheduana of Sumer

1500–1400 B.C.
Hatshepsut of Thebes, Egypt

1200–1100 B.C.
Deborah and Jael of Israel

800–700 B.C.
Semiramis of Assyria

600–500 B.C.
Sappho of Lesbos, Greece

400–300 B.C.
Hipparchia of Athens

100 B.C.–THE YEAR 1 B.C.
Cleopatra Seven of Egypt
Iaia of Cyzicus
Hortensia of Rome

THE YEAR 1 A.D.–100 A.D.
Cleopatra Selene of Mauretania
Trung Trac and Trung Nhi of Vietnam
Hedea, Tryphosa, and Dionysia of Tralles
Locusta of Gaul
Mary Prophetissa of Alexandria
Pan Chao of China

200–300 A.D.
Zenobia of Palmyra

~~~~~~